SELF HELP

SELF HELP

FIND YOUR **SELF** TO HELP YOURSELF

MAX KIRSTEN

HAY HOUSE

Australia • Canada • Hong Kong • India
South Africa • United Kingdom • United States

First published and distributed in the United Kingdom by:
Hay House UK Ltd, 292B Kensal Rd, London W10 5BE. Tel.: (44) 20 8962 1230;
Fax: (44) 20 8962 1239. www.hayhouse.co.uk

Published and distributed in the United States of America by:
Hay House, Inc., PO Box 5100, Carlsbad, CA 92018-5100. Tel.: (1) 760 431 7695 or (800) 654 5126;
Fax: (1) 760 431 6948 or (800) 650 5115. www.hayhouse.com

Published and distributed in Australia by:
Hay House Australia Ltd, 18/36 Ralph St, Alexandria NSW 2015. Tel.: (61) 2 9669 4299;
Fax: (61) 2 9669 4144. www.hayhouse.com.au

Published and distributed in the Republic of South Africa by:
Hay House SA (Pty), Ltd, PO Box 990, Witkoppen 2068. Tel./Fax: (27) 11 467 8904.
www.hayhouse.co.za

Published and distributed in India by:
Hay House Publishers India, Muskaan Complex, Plot No.3, B-2, Vasant Kunj, New Delhi – 110
070. Tel.: (91) 11 4176 1620; Fax: (91) 11 4176 1630. www.hayhouse.co.in

Distributed in Canada by:
Raincoast, 9050 Shaughnessy St, Vancouver, BC V6P 6E5. Tel.: (1) 604 323 7100;
Fax: (1) 604 323 2600

© Max Kirsten, 2011

The moral rights of the author have been asserted.

The author of this book does not dispense medical advice or prescribe the use of any technique
as a form of treatment for physical or medical problems without the advice of a physician, either
directly or indirectly. The intent of the author is only to offer information of a general nature
to help you in your quest for emotional and spiritual wellbeing. In the event you use any of
the information in this book for yourself, which is your constitutional right, the author and the
publisher assume no responsibility for your actions.

A catalogue record for this book is available from the British Library.

ISBN 978-1-84850-253-6

Printed and bound in Great Britain by
TJ International, Padstow, Cornwall.

CONTENTS

Part Four:
THE POWER OF BEING POSITIVE

Part Five:
LIVING LIFE FROM NOW

'Take care of yourself and your Self will take care of you.'

Dedicated to my mother Rosemary, I so wish you could hold this book in your hands. Thank you for everything you gave me.

'Max Kirsten's unique method of hypnotherapy was absolutely key in getting me off cigarettes. His technique is totally effective for many issues and I am sure this book will be a very useful extension of his good work.'

Ewan McGregor

FOREWORD

Congratulations on having bought this extraordinary book.

Like everyone else – me included – you have spent your life searching for love and happiness. Perhaps, like many of us, you have attached your feelings of wellbeing, worth and confidence to things and people outside yourself.

And they were never enough.

So often, it takes a life-crisis to force us to take a few deep breaths and search within ourselves for the answers.

That's when the magic happens, and we find ourselves on a path that empowers us: we find that feelings of worth, security and love are best found within ourselves.

We discover that everything we have ever done, good and bad, has been part of that quest, and that this will always be a journey of imperfection… and that that's OK!

I am often amazed that in a child's literally thousands of hours of formal classroom education, there is rarely even *one* hour of emotional education!

Where *are* the classes on assertiveness or negotiating skills; both requisites for life and for loving relationships?

As for spiritual education, well, I guess there are religious classes, but that is not what I mean: where are the teachers to help us to be our authentic selves, to meditate, to connect with ourselves and others, to find peace?

And if we cannot find peace within ourselves, how do we find it in the world? If we are not settled within ourselves, how can we be settled with another?

This is why we need teachers like Max.

This is no straightforward self-help book. Max does take us through many of the therapeutic processes he himself has used – and they work, if you work them. But this book is also part autobiography, and Max recounts with vivid honesty his own journey from hell to wholeness.

I do hope that you, like me, find much to love about this book.

Charles Montagu

Charles Montagu is Vice-President of the American Council of Hypnotist Examiners (A.C.H.E.) International Division. He is the founder of and practises at the Health Partnership, an integrated medical and holistic practice in South Kensington that combines Western and Eastern approaches to health and wellbeing. He sits on both the Advisory and Examining Boards of the American Council (A.C.H.E), as well as on the Board of the British Council for Complementary Medicine.

ACKNOWLEDGEMENTS

To Siggy, my father and best friend, thanks for everything that you do and 'are'. To my fabulous, Oscar-nominated wife Rebecca and our wonderful son Mylo (who is a constant source of pure amazement). To Wendy and Dudley (my amazing in-laws), whose kind support and love helped me beyond measure.

Thanks to Owen Smith who helped me write and edit this book – we made the journey together.

To my wonderful friend and mentor Charles Montagu CHt. Thanks to my literary agent Robert Kirby and to Lindy King, at United Agents, for all the support. To Michelle Pilley, Jo Lal, Jo, Jessica, Amy and all at Hay House. To Sarah Vine, Sacha Bonser and Penny Walk at *The Times* newspaper. To Rebecca Brooks. To Emillie McMeekan at *The Standard*. To Paul McKenna, Richard Bandler, Dr Brian Roet, Roger Callahan and to William Broom at the General Hypnotherapy Register (GHR), and to all those who trained me.

Special thanks to Ewan McGregor, Dougray Scott, Joseph Fiennes, Bono, Marco Pierre White, Peter Andre, Deirdre Bounds, Peter Maxwell-Lyte, Karen Colognese, Craig and Rachel Ray, Apps Pete NZ, Magnus Fiennes, Olly Meacock, Andy Carroll, Gerry Weatherley, Dr James Ohen-Dejan, John Oakley, my PA Skye Letty, the special Beverly and Juliet Goss, Irving Goldin and his team at Goldin and Co, and to Nigel and all the nurses and staff at the extraordinary Trinity Hospice Xxx. To my great friends Frank Palamara, Shane Desai, Simon Mayle, Ian MacArthur, Howard Napper, Charlotte Di Vita MBE and to all my other close and wonderful friends – you all know who you are. To all at iTunes and Audible.com, and to all the people who have written all the amazing 5-star reviews for my various apps on iTunes – Thanks!

INTRODUCTION

'Who looks outside, dreams; who looks inside, awakens.'

CARL JUNG

If you've picked up this book, then you're probably looking for answers to questions in your life. And there may be a part of you that's wondering if this is yet another 'self-help' book just like all the others. If you're willing to look a little deeper, perhaps you'll find the right answers.

A good friend of mine told me how she used to spend endless hours browsing the 'self-help' section in her local bookshops and on Amazon. She built up an enormous self-help library but found her life didn't change that much. The thing is she never really used any of the books – she never got deeply into them, and in return they never got deeply into her. She admitted she became a 'self-help junkie' – a seeker after all the facts she could muster even though she never actually acted on any of them. The result of all her books was nil because she never properly read and reread them. Somehow she didn't – or couldn't – put the transformational knowledge they contained into action.

This book is different to others, not least because it's backed up by complimentary hypnotic downloads you can get from my website (you can start using these to help you accelerate personal change as soon as you like). I sincerely hope that the book will become a 'must-have' accessory for anyone seriously looking to straighten out, clarify and transform their life. There's so much great information distilled into it – based on my own personal experience and the experience of countless others who have passed this way before – that I hope it's going to end up looking like a well-worn companion on your bookshelf, because it's become the main manual for the most important 'work in progress' in your life – YOU!

> *'If you put a small value upon yourself, rest assured that the world will not raise your price.'*
>
> ANONYMOUS

I believe you owe it to yourself to commit to the simple yet extraordinary process outlined in these pages. The results you desire and dream of await your complete willingness to go to any lengths to make them real. And if you do the work involved you'll be amazed before you're even halfway through.

The great spiritual teachers have said that we can find the answers to everything we need to know within ourselves. But if you're anything like I used to be, you may be looking inside but finding it very hard to see anything at all.

Based on my own experiences – both as a hypnotherapist and as someone coming to embrace self-help from a very uncomfortable place – this book will help you to look deeper within to find a part of you that can provide both inner support and a guidance system that will point you in the right direction. It'll give you the clarity and intuition to keep on the path towards the life you'd like to be living, and the peace of mind to enjoy the journey itself.

This book will help you improve the quality and meaning of your life and offer you the opportunity for deep and permanent transformational change. It can help you to help yourself get past all the things that stand in the way of you becoming the person you're meant to be to fulfil your true potential.

Until I was truly able to find myself, I spent a lot of time being my own worst enemy. Since then, in my therapy practice, I've met so many people in a similar situation. It's made me realize how common this is.

If that sounds familiar, isn't it time you became your own best friend instead of being your own worst enemy?

Don't be like Samantha, in her thirties and on a full-out quest for both 'inner' and 'outer' lightness and wellbeing. She felt she was overweight and was always worried about her appearance. She also recognized that she suffered from low self-esteem and felt compelled to 'improve' herself. The reality was that she was a beautiful woman to look at, but a mass of contradictions on the inside. When we started working together I introduced her to a lot of the things you're going to learn from this book.

And what's she like today? Much happier – because she's using the insights, exercises and techniques on a daily basis; listening to my downloads and acting as a great referrer of clients to me. In fact, she was one of my inspirations for writing this book for you. And she was never an addict of any kind – demonstrating that this book is appropriate for everyone who wants to know what they need to do to help themselves.

This book will help you find the unlimited power and resources that are hidden deep within – and even help you to find a friend or ally in that power.

It was through my introduction, in the early 1980s, to a variety of 12-step fellowships that I was first able to see this extraordinary power at work in the members of these various recovery groups.

Some people call the power 'God', 'Jehovah', 'Allah' or 'The Higher Power', 'Nature', 'The Universe' or 'The Great Spirit'. Diehard atheists involved in the various 12-step programmes often call it the 'power of the group', or 'Good Orderly Direction'

– G.O.D. It doesn't matter how you want to label it; drawing on this unseen power enables your willpower to become enhanced and extraordinary. And, throughout history, human beings have been accessing it to achieve seemingly miraculous results.

The first and probably most important of the 12 steps to recovery involved me having to acknowledge that I had a serious addiction to drugs and alcohol which I was completely powerless to overcome relying on my willpower alone. It wasn't difficult to own up to this, as I'd tried to take back control of my life before and been failing for years. The second step involved acknowledging a power greater than myself which could help me overcome all the problems I was experiencing and even restore me to sanity.

So whether I believed in God or was agnostic or even an atheist, it didn't matter. What *did* matter was my willingness to begin a powerful programme that had worked for countless others since Alcoholics Anonymous was first created by two 'hopeless' alcoholics – Bill W and Dr Bob – in Akron, Ohio in 1935.

Inspired by Bill W and Dr Bob's positive examples, and as their own lives became transformed, the first 100 members collectively wrote the seemingly divinely inspired *Alcoholics Anonymous: the Story of How More than One Hundred Men Have Recovered from Alcoholism* – known informally as the 'Big Book' – somehow creating in the process the miraculous, life-changing 12-step programme to carry the message of recovery to all alcoholics. Since then their programme has been adopted by myriad other addiction-based conditions, creating literally millions of recovery groups all over the world. Henry Kissinger called Alcoholics Anonymous 'the greatest social and spiritual movement of the 20th century'.

Having experienced the extraordinary transformational power available through the 12 steps and having myself been given – seemingly by grace – the 'gift of recovery', I now regularly apply the essence of this spiritual recovery programme in my work as a therapist.

Combining elements of the 12 steps with hypnotherapy and neuro-linguistic programming (NLP) techniques, blended with wisdom I've drawn from other personal development systems and spiritual practices, I've developed an approach to help deal with the full range of regular 'real-life' difficulties we experience in our modern and stressful 21st-century world. These include anxiety, depression, insomnia, self-consciousness, self-centredness, low self-esteem, lack of confidence, addictive behaviours (which can include shopping), escapism and procrastination – through to fully-blown chronic addictions at the extreme end of the spectrum.

When we've got problems that are preventing or blocking us from living the lives we'd like to be living, and stopping us from being the person we'd like to be, willpower alone is often not enough to achieve the permanent transformational change needed to resolve our issues fully.

Sometimes we can become so entrenched in unhealthy behaviours and patterns that real change can seem almost impossible. To realize lasting positive change, finding your deeper inner Self – and the power that comes with that discovery – can become 'the difference that makes the difference' between moving towards where you want to be or remaining annoyingly stuck, just going round and round in circles in a frustrating loop.

Although this book doesn't claim to offer a cure for chronic addictions, I believe it can offer additional advanced support and act as a supplement for people involved in 12-step recovery programmes. I'd seriously recommend that if anybody reading this has deeply rooted addiction issues they consider with an open mind becoming involved with one of these. (I've included a list of 12-step fellowships at the back of the book.)

HOW CAN WE ACHIEVE LASTING CHANGE?

Though we may have the best willpower in the world, it's likely we'll revert to previous 'settings' again and again until we're able to fully reprogramme ourselves to behave as a new person. As a clinical hypnotherapist I understand the potential for using the hypnotic trance-state to create the optimal conditions for faster and deeper, lasting transformation.

We naturally go in and out of trance-states – or altered states of consciousness – all the time. Healing through the trance-state is among the oldest phenomena known to humanity, and is found in one form or another in virtually every culture throughout the world. Even animals are known to go into trance-states.

As I mentioned before, this book comes with the option to get my FREE mind-reprogramming self-hypnosis download to support and complement the exercises I'll be introducing you to a little later. I've created it specially to accompany this book. To access the program simply visit www.maxkirsten.com/selfhelpbook. Enter your details and I'll send you complimentary access. Regularly listening to this hypnotic programme will help you 'fast-track' your transformational change. It'll empower you to help yourself.

> Remember, all real change begins from within. And if you look a little deeper within you'll find your innermost Self – and in that discovery the power to become who you really want to be.

HOW I CAME TO WRITE THIS BOOK – MY OWN SELF-HELP

Ultimately, it's only really you who can help yourself.

Even with all the help in the world, you'll only be able to get so far until you're ready to take full responsibility for doing the work.

Self-help is about giving up blame, because blame takes away your power. Blame turns you into a victim. Self-help is about being grown up and finally taking responsibility for yourself. It's about empowering yourself.

About ten years ago I was at the end of the road. I felt like my life was over. Looking back now, I realize that I was actually at the turning-point to a totally new life. I had finally hit a new rock-bottom – yet again – and was desperate enough and, finally, ready to go to any lengths to turn my life around.

Now I'm running a successful central London therapy practice as a clinical hypnotherapist, master practitioner of NLP, addiction specialist and self-help personal development coach. I'm also selling my 'Max Kirsten' iPhone, iPad and iPod apps on iTunes, audible.com and Google Android – and MP3 hypnosis downloads through my website – all over the world. I've lectured to corporations, been on TV in the UK and the US, been in the press and on radio, and have now written my first book.

And all because I was able to turn my life around, with help from the inside and support from my friends and allies on the outside.

WHAT MAKES THIS BOOK DIFFERENT?

So, given that ultimately you've got to do it for yourself, what can this book offer you – and what makes it any different from the many other books on a similar theme?

First, this book is *authentic*. It's based on my own true 'back from the brink' survivor's experience. Having really been there and done it, I've come back having learned some of the best self-help principles and have combined these with the latest advances in hypnotic mind reprogramming available today. Secondly, this book also represents a distillation of all the self-help principles and techniques which I've personally found completely invaluable and which I'd like to share with you.

The idea of helping yourself can seem a bit paradoxical. On the one hand it might seem to suggest a self-centred or self-preoccupied way of living that's more geared towards satisfying *want* than *need*, and rather suited to our increasingly selfish society. Focused externally on things, and based on what I call 'Moreism' – this kind of 'helping yourself' involves seeking external solutions for internal problems. It's the kind of so-called self-help that's probably got a lot to do with the mess the human race is in today and which we in the West have inflicted and spread by example across the rest of the planet.

On the other hand, the idea of helping yourself takes on a very different flavour if the focus is internal and on those aspects of ourselves that often seem to be so elusive yet have so much of an impact, shaping who we are and how we live our lives.

By helping yourself in the ways I suggest in this book, you're going to give yourself a big step up to living in a better and more harmonious way with the people, places and things around you.

It's often said that you need to be able to help yourself before you can help others; I believe this is true. A good example is the way we're warned in the pre-flight emergency presentation to make sure we've got our *own* oxygen masks on before trying to help anyone else with theirs. You've got to be able to help yourself before you can be an effective help to anyone else.

My hope is that you'll be able to use the various exercises, insights and anecdotes in this book to live a better life from within and find the perfect balance between being both other-centred and 'Self' centred, rather than just being self-centred.

A BIT ABOUT ME

During the first few decades of my life I didn't really pay much attention to helping myself in a particularly constructive way. Growing-up in London in the 1970s, surrounded by the rock-chic of swinging Chelsea's King's Road, I got caught up taking all the recreational drugs I could get my hands on. As a teenager it seemed normal to 'take a walk on the wild side' every day.

Smoking grass and hashish, taking speed, tripping on LSD and magic mushrooms and drinking disturbingly excessive amounts of alcohol, by the time I was in my mid-teens I was well on the way to hedonistic oblivion.

Under the surface I didn't really know what was going on, but then 'under the surface' wasn't a place I thought I needed to pay much attention to. I was having too much fun helping myself to get as high and intoxicated as I could, as often as I could. My mantra back then was, 'Every day's a good day to get high' – and soon enough being normal or 'straight' without the use of drugs just seemed dull and boring.

By my late teens I'd developed a serious dependency on a variety of Class A pharmaceuticals, starting with cocaine and then even onto heroin, plus various other Class B and C recreational drugs – just like the many rock stars of the time. I got a place at St Martin's School of Art, but by then I was really an addict. I was unteachable, arrogant, frustrated, semi-deluded and feeling thwarted at every turn. Sadly, I left before finishing my degree and flew off to New York City to find myself, be found, get rich or die trying. But after a long drug-fuelled year working in New York's top nightclubs in the early eighties, my health was left in shreds and my life completely on the rocks.

With bronchial pneumonia and glandular fever and no proper health insurance, I had to fly back to London for medical attention and straight away got admitted to the Brompton Chest Hospital. I remember walking the length of a single street and feeling completely exhausted. All I could say about anything at that time was 'I just don't know any more.' I felt beaten, baffled, broken, depressed and dramatically suicidal.

After the come-down from all the New York drugs I'd been taking on a nightly basis – including dope, coke, speed, vast amounts of alcohol and MDA (which I really liked – it was the precursor to MDMA/ecstasy and the New York pleasure drug of the early 1980s). My total absorption in unadulterated hedonism ended with me being in a really bad physical and mental state.

Returning to London battered and broken, my parents took me to see a top drugs and alcohol addiction specialist. He recommended two options: being admitted as an in-patient to a very tough, scary-sounding rehab unit near Bristol, or the more gentle-sounding daily attendance at 12-step recovery meetings.

The first choice seemed completely terrifying, so I chose the second.

Attending these extraordinary recovery group meetings, I was surprised to meet people from all different walks of life who were in so many ways just like me but, amazingly, now alcohol- and drug-free, and all seemingly happy. I was more than intrigued, so I got involved and before long it started working for me, too.

I stopped getting loaded and actually started to recover.

Getting involved with 12-step programmes in 1983 gave me the tools I needed to help me to get clean and stay clean and sober, one day at a time. No more the daily self-medicating indulgences of my entire teens and earliest twenties. I was now 23 and beginning a new life in recovery.

Life was scary, exciting, a bit overwhelming – but drug-free. With the support of the programme I didn't take any mind-altering stimulants for about seven years. I got totally fit. I was creative. I started to get work as an art director. I fell in love. Life was good. I worked the Program. I did as advised, and got what the people I'd met had got: a new alcohol- and drug-free life. Life was good.

The 12-step programmes work – it's a fact. But I didn't stick to their simple suggestions, and so for one reason or another – and I really didn't see it coming – I slid back down the slippery slope. It doesn't work if you don't work it.

For one reason or another I started to feel that my life had become difficult. The UK was in a recession and both my love life and my finances were not looking good. As I was reaching my thirties I was feeling a little less than happy with the way things were going. I was feeling restless, irritable and discontented. Out one night at a house-music club, a DJ offered me a puff on a joint. In the darkness, and without a moment's thought, I smoked some of it, and in doing so lit the blue touchpaper to another decade of drug-fuelled hedonistic adventure, and a whole new chapter of addiction.

Before long I was fully back out once again pursuing the rarefied heights of chemical pleasure. I got into taking ecstasy, smoking spliff and snorting coke. I kidded myself I'd be OK as long as I didn't take any opiates, and I promised myself that I wouldn't.

Eventually, though, I started chasing all sorts of dragons in pursuit of the highest of times. But, unlike the last time, at this point in my life I was a now a successful adult with money to burn – uh oh! But, like I'd always done before, I felt lucky. It probably had a lot to do with the arrogance of youth, only this time round I wasn't quite so young.

Compared to a lot of addicts, I was relatively fortunate. I was successfully managing a number of my own businesses: I part-owned a premium rate telecoms business; I was jointly running a successful dance-music nightclub in Berkeley Square, called Club Circa, with my two old friends Rusty Egan and Carol Hayes; I was producing my own brand of deep house trance music, mixing videos and self-medicating with some of the finest grade recreational narcotics in town, 24/7. Hello, London! Lost weekends and blackouts became regular and quite normal.

I was a fully functioning addict but in a slowly descending addictive spiral. I took drugs everywhere I went and on a regular basis, even through international airports. Being somewhere without them was not an option. I was taking greater and greater risks. And then my addictions started to bite back.

As my appetite for stimulants grew out of control, I found I also needed to use something else to take the edge off the industrial quantities of ecstasy and cocaine I seemed to be doing. I started to develop an addiction to over-the-counter, and then prescription painkillers, including codeine of various types. I quickly became dependent on these, then on stronger forms of opiates and then I started chasing the dragon. It was like I was in a movie. I was smoking ever-increasing amounts of heroin and then also taking methadone in pill form. Never one to do things by half-measures, I was unable to stop.

In one of my more lucid moments I remember thinking 'getting off all this stuff is going to be a nightmare.' When I was younger, I kind of thought I was immortal, but now as I was getting older, the true horror of what I'd got myself back into was starting to dawn on me, horribly. Taking more drugs seemed like the best way to shut out those disturbing thoughts. Dig yourself a little deeper, why don't you? There's a saying: 'When you're in a hole, stop digging,' but I just carried on.

Then a series of drug-induced near-death experiences at the end of the 1990s and on the eve of the Millennium took me right to the brink and forced me to acknowledge that I was in a process of total self-destruction. Looking out over the abyss, I realized that it'd been me who'd pushed myself to that dizzying and terrifying edge, and that I was the only person who was going to be able to pull myself back from it.

I was petrified and really didn't want to die. If I was going to live I was going to have to 'clean up' again, but this time with medical help and once and for all. I was going to have to face up to all the things in me that had brought me to that point. It had been me who had helped myself get to where I was, and it was going to have to be me who helped myself back.

So what went wrong the first time round? I'd done the self-help thing and then returned full circle to narco-nihilism. How had that happened?

I'd stopped working the Program. I'd started feeling resentful about one thing and another. My life seemed to me to have got increasingly difficult and I was feeling bad inside. I'd stopped going to 12-step meetings and wasn't looking after my inner condition. I'd split up with my fiancée, was down and depressed and unable to see that, one way or another, most of my problems were of my own making.

I'd gone from self-medication in my youth to self-care in my early twenties, and then back again to self-medication in my early thirties. How could I have let this happen? I had to admit I was powerless over my addictions.

Addiction is a recognized disease. Yet with the right treatment and approach it can be arrested, one day at a time. Combined with an extraordinary inner shift, it is possible to stop the cycle of dependence. I know, because I've done it. Being able to stop something as strong as that cycle has given me the belief that it's possible to achieve far beyond the limited expectations we often set for ourselves.

SELF-HELP AND SELF-CARE

I recognize I've got an addictive personality – for me, it's all or nothing. Looking back, I realize I'm very lucky to be alive, and self-care has been one of the keys to my staying on this path, keeping me doing what I need to do to stay well and practising the spiritual principles I've learned along the way.

For my long-term survival, recovery and self-care had to become a way of life and an attitude of mind. Looking after myself is part of my long-term self-care strategy. My particular journey to self-help was along the path of recovery. Staring out over the abyss, I knew I wanted to be alive long enough to play the long game. After all, I've always loved living life to the full. I didn't want to die of a drug overdose or in an accident.

The final few weeks of my descent were not pretty, big or clever. I'd lost nearly 3 stone in weight; I was emaciated and looked terrible.

Coming off all the drugs in detox I could hardly sit on a chair, concentrate on anything or even breathe properly. Part of me wanted to get well and to be a better person somehow, and another part of me didn't.

Somehow or other I stuck it out and did what had to be done, and I owe a great deal to the medical team, all the other in-patients and the extremely patient hospital bus drivers who drove me and my fellow 'inmates' to a number of local 12-step meetings when we'd finished the clinical detoxification.

For me, it all began there. I had to accept that I had the disease of addiction and that a medical 'cure' didn't exist – but that a new, clean way of life was possible, one day at a time and for as long as I could avoid looking for a pill, powder, toke, smoke or drink.

Fully accepting my problems put me on the path to recovery, but choosing recovery wasn't a quick fix. It's generally true that if you've got an issue you want to overcome, you've got to keep working on it. To benefit fully, self-care has to become part of you and your everyday routine. It's the internal daily workout you do on a regular basis, like cleaning your teeth, doing the housework and taking out the rubbish. It's about replacing a negative internal voice with a positive internal dialogue. It's about changing a bad attitude to a PMA – 'positive mental attitude'. It's about practising the attitude of gratitude. It's a process that has to become your life's work.

BEING 'CLEAR'

To find your Self you have to look within, but sometimes it can be really hard to see beneath the surface. First, you've got to become *clear*.

I've based my approach to self-help in this book on my own experiences and the discoveries and insights I've had on my journey. It's a combination of therapeutic exercises and techniques that I've learned during my recovery and which I've developed and now use as part of my practice as a therapist. Helping others to get on their own paths to becoming clear feels like a privilege – it fulfils and inspires me.

However, having addiction problems is definitely not a prerequisite for using my self-care approach. I've found that this approach is just as effective for people who experience issues such as anxiety, stress, insomnia and phobias – as well as people caught up in self-medicating cycles of addiction. Essentially it's about becoming better at being yourself – to be a complete human being and not just a human doing.

> Learning how to just 'be' is central to my approach.

Developing and following my approach has brought me to where I am now – experiencing a deep and ongoing sense of wellbeing and connectedness to myself and the world, which makes me feel whole. Practising self-care stops me from ever wanting to go back to my old self-medicating ways, keeps me on my path and gives me an illuminated and positive perspective on my past from the warmth and comfort of living each day in what I can only describe as living in 'the sunlight of the spirit'.

- It's all about clearing the negative past to live in the present with the right frame of mind to create the future you want.

- It's about what you're putting into life rather than what you're taking out of it.

- It's about you identifying your unique role in the world and finding your unique place.

- It's about your recognizing your individual value to the human species.

We're all at different places on life's continuum, and ultimately the only person who can take us to where we'd like to be – if we could only get past all the things that hinder us and hold us back – is ourselves.

> *'We don't see things as they are –*
> *we see them as we are.'*
>
> ANAÏS NIN

You've got to find your Self in order to help yourself clear the stuff of the past that's obscuring the reality of the extraordinary present moment.

It's all happening now. And when we're truly clear, we're able to fully experience the wonder of it all in the moment – as it actually is.

It's not where you've been that matters, but where you are and where you're going. How you are now is how you are on your journey to wherever it is you're heading. Being able to take care of yourself and have your Self help you in the present is your key to your excellent unfolding future. And you need real clarity to help you do that.

So, the question is: Are you clear?

If the answer is 'No,' this book will be a guide for you to find that deeper part of yourself which will bring a sense of clarity to your life.

I've heard it said that finding it is 'an inside job'.

I've also heard it said that it's a journey requiring three things: 'change, change, and change' but not necessarily in that order!

- Are you ready to help yourself?

- Are you ready to ask your Self to help you?

- Are you willing to go to ANY lengths to make this work? To make whatever changes are needed to get the life you want? To take responsibility for making the process work one day at a time?

If you are, read on and find out ...

PART 1

RELEASING THE POWER OF THE NEGATIVE PAST

As humans, we have an incredible capacity to learn and grow from everything we experience. In fact our whole survival and evolution as a species depends on our ability to maximize this capacity, and also on our ability to make things happen for us rather than simply have them happen to us.

As individuals, our personal evolution also depends on this capacity to learn from experience. Sometimes, though, rather than making us grow, some things that happen have totally the opposite effect – impacting negatively on us and making us shrink within.

Rather than being able to assimilate new learning and move forward, our experiences often end up being filtered through the effects previous negative experiences have left us with, keeping us stuck in a negative loop.

Everything in life can be an opportunity for learning, even negative experiences. But until we can process negative experiences with clarity, insight and rigorous self-honesty, the potential for learning, and for adding to our lives from that learning, is going to be limited.

'Don't let one cloud obliterate the whole sky.'
ANAÏS NIN

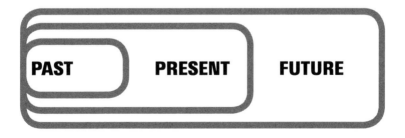

When we're young we're like sponges, absorbing and experiencing everything in the world 'full-on' and directly. Children tend to be relatively open and very present. My wonderful three-year-old son literally drinks life in each day. I love to watch him.

He has purity, an unspoilt innocence, a perfect spirit and a wild and vivid imagination that takes him from the real to the imagined in the twinkle of an eye. I often watch in wonder at the way he reacts to everything so spontaneously. Not that I'm really religious, but it's wondrous to behold and makes total sense of Jesus' statement in the Bible:

> *'Let the children come to me… For the Kingdom of God belongs to those who are like these children'*
>
> New Living Translation

This openness has got a double edge, though. When we're children we have a vulnerability that doesn't always help us shrug things off in the same way we might do as we get older.

As with everything, it's all relative and some of us are more susceptible than others to absorbing the daily hurts and slights life brings. What Shakespeare called 'the slings and arrows of outrageous fortune' either bounce off or embed themselves. And when we're young we don't necessarily have the skills or perspective to deal with this.

Looking back, I think I was probably one of those susceptible, open, positive children who tended to get spiked by the arrows and slings. And looking back, maybe the enthusiasm with which I embraced new opportunities for getting 'high' in my early teens was my way of dealing with those bad feelings, by 'self-medicating'.

The secondary school I went to when I was 11 was quite tough. I had some really bad experiences and in my first year suffered the humiliation of getting beaten up a few times. Those experiences definitely left their mark, making me feel like I'd been reduced as a person.

How experience impacts on us is relative to our individual characters, personalities and innate coping mechanisms. I was an only child and very close to my parents. Though in my home life I was fortunate never to experience any major suffering or abuse, even in that situation things happened that made me shrink on the inside.

As I grew into my teenage years, I noticed an uncomfortable awkwardness in myself, and a growing social phobia. Meeting new people seemed to become harder and I began to feel more and more self-conscious. Of course, these feelings are fairly normal for teenagers, but back then all I knew was that it made me feel bad. But when I got high on drugs all my frustrations, fears and doubts completely disappeared.

Being stoned or getting high made everything seem possible. 'I want to feel this good every single day, and why shouldn't I?' I used to think. Those were truly the wild and groovy times. Life in the 1970s was fun. 'I really LOVE this!' I thought.

So from my early teens I set about chasing this new way of living. Looking around I noticed that success seemed to come to a lot of people who got high. Artists, writers and rock stars like Picasso, William S Burroughs, Aldous Huxley, The Rolling Stones, The Beatles, Led Zeppelin, Bowie, Bolan – OK, so he died in a car crash... the list went on and on.

As the seventies progressed I started spending more and more time in a drug-induced blur. All I really noticed was how great I felt when I got loaded, but maybe part of me was getting high in order to escape the uncomfortable way I felt inside.

Left unprocessed, and without my realizing it, those uncomfortable feelings were building up into the emotional contents of my negative past. In the following pages I'm going to outline some of the self-help techniques and exercises that helped me get rid of unwanted negative feelings I'd been carrying for a long time.

1

RELEASING THE WEIGHT OF NEGATIVE PAST EXPERIENCE

*'Do not dwell in the past;
do not dream of the future,
concentrate the mind on the
present moment.'*

BUDDHA

Things we've done in the past, and things people have done to us, carry the potential to become baggage. In my case, without my being aware of it, feeling weighed down by all that baggage probably contributed to me spending a whole lot of time getting high. In actuality all I was doing was incrementally adding more and more to the baggage that was already there – layer upon layer.

Eventually I'd amassed enough to fill the entire cargo-hold of a jumbo jet; an emotional and physical crash was inevitable. It could well have been fatal, and I feel incredibly blessed by grace to still be here and able to share this with you.

Picking up the pieces after the crash was a long and often painful process, but up to that point the methods I'd been using to try to ignore my baggage had very nearly led to my complete extinction. The recovery process helped me shape the phoenix I became and set me on the path to achieving a potential light-years beyond my previous junk-addled prospects.

If you want to get on the true path to wellbeing and wholeness – and find essential clarity – there's really no avoiding opening up those old suitcases, trunks and holdalls that we've conveniently misplaced the keys and combinations for.

Excess baggage usually incurs a cost to our emotional wellbeing, and eventually an unavoidable surcharge to our physical health.

> *'You're only as sick as your secrets.'*
> ANONYMOUS

The sooner we take stock and assess the weight we've been carrying from the past into the present, the sooner we can begin to lighten our physical load, let go of the past and shed the burden of our baggage.

THE NEGATIVE INNER VOICE

Unprocessed, the negative past seeps into the present, carried in the backpack of our memories. Its weight may be virtual but its impact can be deep. It certainly shaped the course of my life for a good number of years. One of the ways it afflicted me was through an internal voice continually passing judgement on whatever I was doing or trying to do.

Negative feelings carried from our past often express themselves as accusatory and chastising inner voices that goad and limit us, and hold us back from living to our full potential. These internal negative voices can replay a familiar loop – 'I told you it wouldn't work,' 'You can't do that,' 'You don't deserve it,' 'They're going to find out you're a fake,' 'Forget it, you're not good enough', and so on.

I remember the relief when all those inner demons of self-doubt simply evaporated and dissolved a few moments after smoking a joint. Over time though, as I slowly lost my balance and descended into multiple addictions, the reliable relief from my inner turmoil and that wonderful feeling of instant hedonistic pleasure seemed to get less and less. So I went in search of more.

Much later, as I contemplated the ashes of my old unsustainable, single-minded, self-medicating and self-centred life, I learned to live with those disruptive negative voices and started to formulate a very different relationship with them. Understanding the factors that had led to the voices being there, I learned to ignore their unfounded, fear-based lies. I learned to challenge them with a new inner courage and a quieter but stronger internal voice that said 'I can, I will and I am!' I'll tell you more about the methods I used to do this a little later in the book.

IN THE BEGINNING

'Things do not change; we change.'
HENRY DAVID THOREAU

Personally, I adhere to a belief system that says that essentially at birth we're 'equal to all and second to none'. Of course, the social context we're born into determines where we might fit in socially, but that's not what I'm talking about here. What I'm referring to is the idea that we enter this world with innocence, purity and a completely clean slate.

Though unable to rationalize it in words, as I developed a childish sense of my little universe I became aware of various influences affecting me and the world I was growing into. One of these had to do with how I was being perceived by people I came into contact with. I often wondered what people around me were thinking about me.

An only child, I remember feeling most comfortable when I was either on my own or just with my parents. Without any siblings to learn from, I don't think it's uncommon for only children to sometimes find it a bit of a challenge to get to grips with interacting with other children.

I remember as I got older being encouraged to extend myself beyond my comfort zone and try to make new friends. Sometimes it worked and sometimes I got knocked back. And when that happened, I felt it and it didn't feel good. I hated being outside my own comfort zone and risking being rejected. Taking it to heart, rejections from other kids left me feeling hurt, insecure and wondering if there was perhaps something wrong with me.

What I imagined people thought and felt about me definitely had an impact and influenced how I felt about myself. What I didn't realize was that what people were feeling about me was being influenced by what they felt about themselves. It wasn't until much later, when I began picking through the ashes of my burnt-out past, that I started to appreciate how multilayered our relationships with ourselves and others actually are.

As a child growing up I was always aware of a low-level sense of disquiet; a feeling that something wasn't quite right and that there was something missing. I interpreted this as being to do with me.

In the same way that I don't believe in 'original sin', I also don't believe children are born with an inclination to believe there's something essentially wrong with them. Why would they? They've got nothing to compare themselves to.

Marco Pierre White, a very old friend of mine and now one of the world's greatest living chefs, was once asked by a journalist how he thought growing up on a council estate in Leeds had affected him. He replied, 'I have no idea, because I had nothing to compare it to. It was normal.' It must have had some kind of effect, but having not known anything else he could only guess, but he wasn't going to do that to suit a journalist.

I think the relationships we have with the people who bring us up probably have a greater influence on us than where we are brought up. I also think our early lives are affected by the internal life-maps that our parents carry with them.

MY PARENTS

My mother certainly didn't have an average childhood – if there is such a thing. Born into a family of five children, she was the only one to be fostered out just before the Second World War. She was brought up separated from her parents and siblings. Her early life was shaped through experiences of disappointment, rejection and a deep sense of abandonment. Despite this, and perhaps as a response, she first got a scholarship to a grammar school and, after that, a very rare scholarship to the Central School of Drama (which in those days was at the very top of the Royal Albert Hall's dome). She never looked back.

Being fostered was not something my mother ever went to great lengths to talk about but it must have had an impact on her. When pressed, she would describe herself with a shudder as being what in those days was called a 'home child'. It must have affected her feelings about herself, and had a hand in drawing the map of the world she carried with her subsequently. And it must have affected the way she later related to me and the way she engaged with me as a growing child. Perhaps what you don't know you don't miss, but what you've never had yourself you won't know how to give.

How a young child develops emotionally has to be influenced by the way their parents feel about themselves. And further back, how their parents' parents felt about themselves. Our emotional inheritance, subtle or profound, comes with its own weight and its own positive or negative value.

My mother didn't let her early difficult experiences stop her from achieving personal success. She went on to act, sing and become a model, and she certainly didn't let her feelings push her life into self-induced free-fall like I did. But I wonder how she processed feelings she carried from her childhood. Looking back, I'm sure my mother was emotionally affected by her experience of being unhappily fostered, and I'm also sure that somehow that affected how she related to me when I was a child.

My father also had an unusual childhood. During the Second World War he and his two brothers were evacuated from England to the US, where they grew up in Philadelphia with the well-to-do Packard (as in the car makers) family.

Dad and his two brothers didn't know their own father. He had split from and divorced their mother while she was pregnant with my dad. My father never actually met his father until he was 21 years old. They met for lunch for an hour and it didn't go very well. They never met again.

My father had joined the RAF just before meeting his father, who had been a flying officer in the RAF's 442 Squadron. Later he met my mother and started one of the first swinging-60s boutiques in London. He also became a model and then spent 20 years in advertising. He was one of the very first hand models in Europe, and was the original pilot's hand in the worldwide press and billboard poster campaigns for Rothmans cigarettes – pretty ironic, given his father's career as a pilot. I remember seeing his giant hand, with the pilot stripes of his cuff, holding a massive open pack of cigarettes, literally wherever I went for about 10 years until cigarette advertising was banned. 'That's my dad's hand,' I'd say to friends, pointing up at the huge poster. It was truly bizarre.

It's another irony that he was helping encourage people to smoke. One of my biggest missions is to help as many people on the planet as possible quit smoking, with hypnosis using my downloadable apps. Having just watched my mother die of a smoking-related cancer, I'm even more inspired and determined to fight the fight for freedom from nicotine addiction. And if that's one of your demons, please see my website for more information, help and support.

My father was also the hand in the original 1970s Yellow Pages 'let your fingers do the walking' TV advert. He definitely wasn't the typical career father. Both my father and mother did the most and best they could with little experience of parental role models for themselves. Most of what they had learnt was from movies they'd seen.

The feelings of disquiet I had as a young child were a kind of insecurity, and not 'feeling right' to do with low self-esteem. If as children we don't feel special or valuable, where do these feelings come from? As I've said, I suspect it's most likely from our parents and probably because they didn't feel special or valuable themselves.

It's all about 'past life' stuff, but not in the reincarnation sense. I can see where I may have picked up feelings that dogged me through the first two decades of my life, and particularly low self-esteem and anxiety.

Low self-esteem and a hidden sense of shame are perhaps the biggest obstacles we can face in relation to achieving our true potential. Ironically, I think low self-esteem is often unconsciously instilled in us by our parents, even when they're desperate to encourage just the opposite, knowing the negative effect it's had on them in their lives. Because both my parents had difficult backgrounds, they unsurprisingly found it a challenge to have a balanced relationship with each other. They were prone to regular arguments and tempestuous rows that inevitably affected my sense of security and created the perfect conditions for my insecurity and personal anxiety.

In saying this, I'm not being accusatory nor implying a sense of blame. I love my parents from the bottom of my heart and am deeply grateful to them for my life and their extraordinary contribution to it. I'm just indicating an ongoing legacy that I've found it really useful to identify and acknowledge.

I think Philip Larkin's poem *This Be the Verse* sums it up perfectly. Beginning with the line, 'They fuck you up, your mum and dad – they may not mean to but they do', the poem acknowledges that there's a negative generational effect handed down through families. Personally, I don't have as pessimistic a view as Philip Larkin had. I believe it is possible to clear the negative past we've inherited from our parents through some deep inner work and a greater understanding of how we came to be who we've become.

KNOW YOUR PAST, KNOW YOURSELF

To help yourself you've got to know yourself, and to really know yourself you've got to know your past. Acknowledging your past, how it has contributed to the baggage you're still carrying and how that may still be affecting you, is a leap towards your clarity and freedom.

It's my personal belief that when we're strangers to ourselves there's a danger that we can slowly become mentally, spiritually and even physically unwell. If we have a sense of unease with being alone with ourselves, it's easy to slip into myriad self-soothing and self-medicating addictions – alcohol and drugs, gambling, food disorders, shopping and sex addiction – anything that can take us away, or distract us from the uncomfortable feelings of being with the stranger inside.

But until we're ready to find inside solutions for inside problems, the difficulties we are having are not going to go away.

'When we are unable to find tranquillity within ourselves, it's useless to seek it elsewhere.'
FRANÇOIS DE LA ROCHEFOUCAULD

EXTERNAL FACTORS IN THE NEGATIVE PAST

We are part of two worlds, the external world around us and our personal inner world. Because it's physical and material we can see, hear, touch, smell and taste the external world. The world inside is something we feel. The relationship between the physical world and our inner world shapes us as the individuals and personalities we are, and the way we feel about ourselves shapes how we feel about the world.

The experiences life throws at us have their own influence on the way we are as individuals. And how we feel about the world plays its own part in shaping the experiences life puts our way. It's a complex and multilayered loop, but paying attention to the loop's feedback can give us insights and clues that can support us to start consciously redesigning the person we want to be.

When I began my second recovery after the Millennium, and as part of the process of becoming well, I was encouraged to make a series of lists about myself and my life. I started thinking about the people and events that had had an impact on me in a powerful enough way to lodge themselves in my memory with deep feeling. The lists were drawn up from memories of people and events in which I'd felt hurt, slighted, insulted, humiliated or shamed in one way or another, and also of people that I'd hurt and slighted.

When I was about eight, a boy in my class at school cut my finger, seemingly for fun. I'd rather hated him ever since, despite the fact that I knew he was probably a very troubled soul. There was something about the experience that highlighted a dark and threatening side to life: that people had the potential to hurt me without a second thought.

On my first day in secondary school I got punched in the face by someone who decided they didn't like the look of me. Someone else who made me feel that the world wasn't necessarily the safe place I wanted it to be. Another memory laced with injury and hurt feelings.

Our lives are full of these incidents and events. I count myself fortunate that the things that happened to me were relatively mild in comparison to some of the terrible events, incidents and experiences that many less fortunate people have to go through. I was never badly physically, sexually or emotionally abused. I didn't suffer any extreme physical hardship – until of course my self-created drug addiction which eventually completely enslaved and engulfed me – but still, I managed to amass my own collection of negative baggage.

I remember leaving a newsagent's shop with my mother when I was about six years old. She discovered I'd taken some sweets from the shop's counter. She scolded me and then grabbed me by the hand and marched me back inside to have me give them back and say sorry.

I was embarrassed and felt humiliated and a deep sense of shame. It was a formative memory of my feeling that there was something wrong with me. Of course I needed to learn that what I had done was wrong, but the experience left a negative mark on me and certainly didn't stop me from stealing again in the future.

Despite my mother's attempt to deter me from stealing I spent my early teenage years on an extended spree of compulsive thieving. I wasn't alone, though: shoplifting for fun was a bit of a sport among my peers at school.

As a teenager I was out of control at a school that seemed to be out of control. Teachers used to take the register and mark everyone in as present even if they weren't, I guess because it was easier for them that way. Meanwhile, my friends and I were in the park or on the street, usually up to no good.

I remember thinking it was unfair that people should have things I didn't. I thought that my wanting to have them justified my taking them. And as I seemed to get away with it, I developed the practice like a muscle. I got caught up in a bizarre compulsive cycle of not feeling very good about myself and taking things I wanted because I thought they'd make me feel better, and then feeling uncomfortable for doing it but carrying on doing it anyway.

My bizarre thieving phase went on for some years. It was motivated by my constantly looking at what other people had and seeing that in relation to what I felt I didn't have. Later, as I became more comfortable with looking at my inner world, and was able to spend more time doing that than focusing on the outer world, I had less and less need to look at others and make comparisons based on appearance.

Maybe there could have been other ways for my mother to teach me that what I had done was wrong. Her response was based on what she knew and her vocabulary of possible responses to the situation. She was just doing the best she could based on her own experience and knowledge.

During my recovery I realized how important it was to desist from laying blame. After all, as they say, 'One finger pointing forward leaves three pointing back.' By then I'd become very good at it. I'd spent years carrying the victim's mentality in my collection of baggage, and it took me a while to realize that to avoid being a victim I had to acknowledge the responsibility I had to myself to evolve beyond my experiences in the past.

It's time to forget the blame game and take responsibility for making your life a success. Blame takes away your personal power and turns you into a powerless victim.

> *'When you blame others you give up*
> *your power to change.'*
> ROBERT ANTHONY

Self-help is about taking responsibility for the past and the present, and if you're unhappy with either, taking responsibility to change the circumstances that have led you to feeling unhappy.

Blaming others for difficult circumstances and situations is easy, but the only person we can change is ourselves. The responsibility for making the change lies within ourselves. When I was in the depths of self-destruction, I was the last person I wanted to look at or into. It took me a good while to realize that, deep down, I did have the power to change and that, ultimately, I was the only person I could ever really change anyway.

Ultimately, it was from a point of complete despair, when I was finally 'sick and tired of being sick and tired', that I found the power within that I needed to begin to change. I remember being told that reaching the state of complete desperation was a gift. I've since come to realize how important hitting rock-bottom was, and how important change is.

Ongoing change is the way of the universe. It's a constant process. In an ever-changing world we have to learn to adapt to change. In order to help myself change, I had to embrace this fully.

Embracing change helped me to have a vision of where I wanted to get to, and then to start moving towards it in order to achieve my dream. With a vision of where I wanted to be in my mind, I started trimming my life accordingly, adjusting myself little by little in order to get myself on the path I'm now incredibly grateful to be on.

An awful lot of things happen in the external world that we don't seem to have any control over. If we feel clear on the inside it's a lot easier to process unexpected external events, and to manage change as it happens.

Clear of the clutter of the negative past, we can help ourselves move towards our dreams for the future.

BECOMING CLEAR AND RELEASING THE BLOCKS

As humans, we are far more than just flesh and blood. We've got a mind which, for much of the time, engages in an ongoing conversation with itself, and we have a spirit that expresses something about ourselves beyond the mind's chatter and the body's limitations. There's a connection between each of these, and the relationship we have with each has an effect on the other two.

Carrying a negative past limits our capacity to experience our spirit in its fullness. It blocks out our spirit's 'light' and interferes with our ability to feel comfortable with simply living in the moment.

Resentments, fears, insecurities and feelings of guilt and shame also stop us from being able to enjoy being 'clear and present' in the way we could if we weren't carrying all that internal baggage. Above all, these feelings limit our sense of self-value and esteem. The feelings we carry in our memories have a big influence on how we feel about ourselves and the world and people around us.

We're also the outcome of how we've processed difficult experiences, the slings and arrows that either bounced off, maybe leaving just a scratch or a bruise, or got deeply embedded and absorbed. Our personal insecurities, resentments and fears, those feelings of guilt and shame – feelings that sprang from experience, and which we've packed away and carry with us – all play their part in shaping and influencing who we are today.

I was once in the middle of a social gathering. I wanted to leave the room, and walked up to and opened a door that I thought was the way out. I went through it then suddenly realized I was in a dark cupboard. It could have been really interesting if it was a doorway to Narnia, but it was just a cupboard and I froze with embarrassment.

At the time I was already feeling a bit insecure in the situation. Inside the walk-in cupboard and in the dark I found I couldn't bring myself to walk out and appear like the fool I thought I'd be seen as. I stood there in a minor panic, thinking that the people in the room would laugh at me. The longer I stood in the cupboard the more humiliated and stupid I felt. Finally I emerged – as though I'd been next door or down the corridor – and made a joke of it, laughing and saying that I'd been secretly listening to everyone's conversations.

In retrospect I realize that nobody knew what I had done and had no idea what I was going through. They were all far too interested in talking and thinking about themselves to notice my mistake. It also made me realize how feelings of insecurity can be literally paralysing.

Insecurity can be boiled down to worrying about what other people think about us, and low self-esteem to believing in a distorted image of ourselves and not recognizing the inherent value we carry within.

Self-help is a bit like making sure you're getting a regular personal MOT. It involves making sure you keep a regular check on what's going on inside. It's very important to keep consciously mindful of those negative moments, thoughts and feelings. And when you notice them, to identify where they're coming from and whether they're in response to reality and what's actually happening or are imagined and caused by the baggage of your negative past.

When I'd reached my abyss of deep despair, I was forced to acknowledge that an inner MOT was long overdue. That was my first step towards sorting out the cycle of behaviour that had conditioned my life for years, enabling me to release the blocks that had kept me stuck in self-destructive behaviour. Taking that step allowed me to begin to enjoy a vision of the fundamental beauty of a perfectly imperfect world.

My ability to develop that vision depended on my being able to finally turn the lens on myself and acknowledge my part in everything that had happened in my life. Then I had to release all the things that had led to the negative cycles of behaviour I was more than ready to step out of.

I'd like to introduce you to the process I used to do this.

2

THE FIRST STEPS TO RELEASE

*'Those who are free of resentful
thoughts surely find peace.'*

Buddha

People with addictive personalities really shouldn't take addictive drugs for recreational pleasure.

From collecting comics to sport, I was always a bit obsessive about the things I enjoyed. Some of my passions were harmless and even positive. Addictive behaviour can be channelled to achieve extraordinary things. When I was 15, I became British Junior Frisbee Champion as a result of an obsessive love of throwing Frisbee with people who were really good at it. But by getting loaded every day, I was heading for trouble.

The end of my second path of a life of 24-hour partying was marked by a series of frustrations and deep feelings of pain and suffering. As a result of my various addictions I'd become pretty much broken-down. In the end and in desperation I finally took myself into rehab for a full opiate detox from heroin, methadone and prescribed codeine, various other pills (including Rohypnol), marijuana, cocaine, ecstasy and 40 Marlboro cigarettes a day. As I said before, I don't do half-measures.

While in hospital I was reintroduced to the various 12-step programmes that I'd first come across kicking my drug and alcohol dependencies back in the 1980s. I was told that in order to move beyond where I was, and if I was truly going to begin to recover one day at a time, I needed to do some real work on myself. However, until I was able to work out what needed to be fixed, I was going to remain unfixable. At the time I could barely stay seated on a chair for any longer than a minute.

The various medicinal cookie jars I'd been reaching into, which had ultimately got me into the mess I was in, were no longer an option. It was time to start looking into my own cookie jar, so to speak.

If it's become obvious to you that your life's not going how you want it to go, that maybe things are going downhill fast and there are things you'd really like to change, you're going to have to start looking inside yourself for another way to live.

For me, looking inside was the first stage of my road to recovery.

All my wheels had fallen off and the road I'd been rock-and-rolling along had all but run out and I wasn't going any further. I needed to go back into my life's story, work out how I'd got to where I was, find out what was wrong and find a way to move beyond where I'd ended up.

The first of the 12 steps involves acknowledging that you've got a problem you're powerless to overcome, and that as a result your life has become unmanageable.

How could I have been so stupid, arrogant and deluded to think that taking drugs like 'normal' people, who seemed to be able to take them and leave them, was a good idea? The thing is, I *never* took drugs like normal people. 'Normal' didn't seem to be in my repertoire. I was all or nothing.

The first step of the programme guided me onto the path of recovery. I had to admit to myself that I was beaten and needed super-help.

The second step of the 12-step programme involves acknowledging – believing in or finding – a higher power 'greater than our normal selves' which can 'restore us to sanity' and which has helped countless other people onto the path of successful recovery.

The third step involves making a personal decision to hand over your 'life and your will' into the 'care' of this higher power, whatever your concept of that power is. The third step can be a real challenge if you're not particularly religious or even spiritually minded. Learning to pray like a drowning man or woman is probably a close approximation to the effort and sincerity that can be needed for this step.

The fourth step involved me writing a series of lists to help me understand what was going on inside. From the outset of my recovery, I was encouraged to acknowledge that *I* was probably at the root of my problems.

Until I got involved with the 12 steps, the only lists I'd ever made in my life were what I wanted for Christmas and what stimulants me and my friends planned to get hold of on a day-to-day or week-by-week basis.

Remember, there's really only one person you can change, and that's yourself. The question is, what to change? Your lists are a fact-finding mission.

For me even to contemplate doing this kind of difficult and challenging personal work, I had to be desperate for change to happen. And I was. I really couldn't go on as I had been. I knew I had to change, but I also had to know exactly *what* to change in order to make my recovery permanent.

Learning to make a personal inventory helped me see what I was carrying and to make a link between that and my self-destructive behaviour. It was a profoundly useful exercise, and I'd like to share it with you now.

I hope that you're either smarter than me, and willing to do what it takes without the motivation of 'enough pain and suffering' or, if you're like I was, you've had enough of pain and suffering and are finally ready and willing to go to any length to do the work.

WRITING THE DARK LISTS

'What lies behind us and what lies before us are tiny matters compared to what lies within us.'

RALPH WALDO EMERSON

Who would care to admit their faults and to list all the things about themselves they would rather not see, admit or even think about? Blaming others is far easier than shouldering the blame and taking responsibility for keeping your side of the street clean and up to date. Remember, we are learning a new discipline for a daily programme.

For it to be effective, making a personal inventory requires following each of the stages I'm going to outline. Doing this will enable you to experience the full value of the exercise once you've done it. It's a bit like regularly doing the housework and then being able to enjoy having a clean house once it's all finished. It should mark the beginning of a lifelong process that'll support your wellbeing on your journey to come.

In order to do this exercise, you're going to need an A4 pad, exercise book or similar. It's probably a good idea to read through the instructions first and to familiarize yourself with what to do before you start writing. It's probably also a good idea to find a quiet place where you're not going to be disturbed and where you feel comfortable and at relative peace.

If you can, I'd recommend that you make all your lists ideally over one weekend, with lots of breaks to go for walks, get fresh air and see the ever-changing sky. If you can't do it like this and need to spread the task out, each time you come to the exercise you should give yourself a clear stretch of time, say at least 30 minutes.

I'd also recommend that when you write the lists, you do them in your best handwriting. Typing them just doesn't feel quite the same. It's somehow less physically and mentally engaging; writing things out by hand is more personal, natural and, most of all, spiritually connecting. There's a link between what you bring up from your subconscious mind, let travel down your arm and onto the page. It completes a natural and organic journey from the unconscious to the conscious and has its own spiritual quality.

Clear your mind and ask it to help you remember all the relevant details you're looking for. It's definitely NOT a good idea to leave your pad or exercise book lying around for anyone else to read. Treat your lists as strictly private and confidential, and even sacred.

THE INVENTORY OF RESENTMENTS

Divide a blank page into three columns.

Take a few deep breaths and turn your attention to yourself and your past.

In the first column – and working forward in time – list all the people you have ever felt resentment towards.

It can help if you work in five- or seven-year segments. Start with the first segment of your life then move onto the next and so on, right up to the present day.

Cast your mind right back to the earliest memories you can recall.

Scanning these bite-sized chunks of your life, in the first column list all the people that you've ever felt aggrieved by and that – for whatever reason – you've felt or feel resentful towards. Make a note of anyone you've encountered that you feel you've been hurt by, and as a result felt some form of resentment towards.

Even though these resentments aren't necessarily on the surface of your conscious awareness in your daily life, if you can remember them when you dig into the past they're still there. The rule of thumb is, if you still remember things they ARE important, so, methodically, get them all down on paper.

If, with a little effort, you're able to remember them, they're still polluting your inner world and preventing you from enjoying being yourself now, as much as you could be without that internal pollution. Clearing the past's negative influence on the present is a crucial first step on the path to self-help and greater clarity.

In her wonderful book *Fulfilled – A Personal Revolution in 7 Steps*, Deirdre Bounds gives a very clear definition of what the word 'resentment' actually means and how it can affect us.

'So, what is resentment? Well, let's look at the Latin root of the word with the prefix, *re*, and *sentire*, which means to 're-feel'. So it is to re-feel a wrongdoing. If you think that someone or something has done you wrong then you replay that feeling of bitterness, indignation or anger in your mind like an old record that's stuck. And if that's not bad enough, you then get a perverted delight in not only thinking about it but telling others about it... Every time you tell the story of the wrongdoing, you 're-feel' it and, although you're trying to get it off your chest, it doesn't go away, in fact it feels even worse and to cap it all you get a sick sort of satisfaction out of your victimhood.'

Old and festering resentments stop us from living in a clear state in the present, and prevent the inherent light of our spirit from shining through.

Resentments we're carrying in the backpacks of our memories will subconsciously help shape the way we relate to people in the present moment. We're likely to find ourselves responding in particular ways to people we meet who appear to act in a similar way to people from our past that we're still carrying negative feeling towards. Rather than responding openly to what's happening in the moment, we're likely to let our responses be shaped by memories of resentments and old hurts still seeping through and influencing us.

As well as the store manager who you had a flaming argument with over a return, there may also be people on your list whom you've felt resentful towards at some time or other but who you also care about – your mother and father, siblings, partners, relatives and old friends.

In the second column – and alongside your list of names – write down what led to the feeling of resentment that you've been carrying in that backpack. What's the reason for this resentment?

My list included things like – my parents for not letting me watch TV programmes I wanted to watch, not giving me a Chopper bike like my best friend's, making me eat food I didn't want to eat; teachers who made me feel like I was stupid; that boy who cut my finger; friends who abandoned me and hurt my feelings; the girl who didn't love me when I loved her – stuff that had happened a long time ago, and could seem inconsequential but which I was still unconsciously carrying around inside.

In the third column – alongside the reason for the resentment – make a note of how the incident affected you. Did it leave you with a physical injury – major or minor – or scar? Did it hurt your pride or otherwise have an impact on you emotionally? Did it undermine your sense of self or your self-esteem?

These old resentments can sometimes be buried quite deeply, so take the time to ask your inner Self or your connection with the higher power to help you while casting your mind back over the landscape of your memory.

Usually the list gathers momentum as you get into your teenage years. You may well begin to see patterns of resentment that have built up for the same or similar things happening again and again. It's quite an illuminating process, going back then tracking forwards from the first few items of baggage in your collection to the present.

You can add to, change or revise your list over time, but initially note down the names, events and their effects that stand out the most for you.

THE INVENTORY OF DARK SECRETS

The next essential list I'd suggest you make is the 'secrets' list. This should be a list of all the things you've done that no one knows about. Things you did that maybe you wish you hadn't, things you've been involved with that you really shouldn't have been. Basically, all the secrets you'd rather take to the grave with you. And don't forget the saying – 'You're only as sick as your secrets!'

It's time to begin the process of cleansing yourself of your dark secrets in order to experience the wonderful sense of wellbeing that'll follow.

Remember to write the list for your eyes only and don't leave it lying around. It's best you find a secure place to keep all these lists, somewhere super-safe. This definitely isn't a list you should leave around the home or office.

To begin, divide a blank page into three columns.

Take a few deep breaths, clear your mind for a few moments and then turn your attention to yourself and your past.

Cast your mind right back to the earliest memories you can recall.

Scanning in five- or seven-year, bite-sized chunks – in the first column list the things that you've done, said or thought that you're carrying around as a guilty secret.

Go back to your earliest memories and track forward, dredging up all the dark secrets that you've kept well hidden.

In the second column make a note of what happened.

In the third column make a note of how the secret makes you feel. This might include guilty, shameful, disgusted, fearful, anxious, dishonest, inferior or ashamed.

Remember, this is a process that you can follow to help yourself achieve greater wellbeing, a clear conscience and clarity. Half-measures will not achieve the desired result. Find the courage, faith and a vision of hope for a better you. These are your drivers for success.

If you get stuck, don't forget the idea of calling on your inner self or the 'power greater than you' to help you with this task.

THE INVENTORY OF REGRETS

Another dark list I'd recommend you make is a list of regrets – the 'if only' list. The point of this list is to find peace with the past – to accept it, no longer have regrets about it and to reach a point where the past is finally over.

Divide a blank page into three columns.

Begin by taking a few deep breaths; turn your attention to yourself and your past.

Tracking forward from your earliest memories – and in five- or seven-year chunks – in the first column make a list of the regrets you carry with you from your past. Beginning with phrases like – 'If only I hadn't said ...', 'If only I hadn't been caught ...', 'If only I hadn't screwed up my ...', 'If only I had ...'

List all those disappointments and regrets.

My 'regrets' list included things like – if only my parents had been better off; if only I hadn't said all those awful things in that peak of rage; if only I hadn't felt the poisonous resentment towards people I really cared about; if only I'd had brothers and sisters; if only I hadn't been sent to that awful secondary school; if only I'd finished my degree at St Martin's.

However trivial it may seem in the light of day, if it's something you regret, include it. If you can remember something and there's even the slightest regret attached to it, it's important and needs to be processed for you to be able to move on.

In the second column make a note of any particular detail you feel is important.

In the third column make a note of how the regret makes you feel.

Remember, we can't undo the past; what's done is done and can't be undone – but we can learn from things we've done and regret doing, or haven't done and regret not doing. It's all too easy to try to bury the past and end up making the same mistakes again, or to distort the past and turn minor glitches into major disasters. Making these lists isn't a conceptual exercise, it's about acknowledging and then changing our behaviour.

Going through our baggage piece by piece, we can learn by looking at its contents before we get rid of it once and for all.

THE INVENTORY OF FEARS

The final dark list I'd suggest you make is the list of fears.

Begin by taking a few deep breaths and then turning your attention towards yourself. When writing this list you should stay in the present and note down all those fears that are currently unsettling you and causing you either major or minor distress.

Spend some time thinking about all those things that are no more than a nagging worry and also things that completely terrify you. List all the fears you carry around with you.

It might be anything from getting cancer, being penniless, losing your home or not achieving a dream to getting old, being lonely or dying alone. List all the fears you're harbouring inside.

What's the opposite of fear for you?

Under your list of fears, make a list of the qualities and strengths that you feel offer an antidote to fear. The list might include faith, hope, courage, light, freedom, peace, spirituality, feeling good, wellbeing and love. Whether it's any or all of these – and others I've not listed – make your own list and begin to focus more and more on these strengths.

Begin to feel them in your life.

Making The Dark Lists will enable you to take charge and play an active role in your release from all your past resentments, secrets, disappointments and fears. The ultimate aim is to put you in a position where you can say that the greatest thing about the past is that it's over and done with.

And it's about doing this for yourself – helping yourself release the negative past to begin to live with clarity in the present.

With fewer and fewer echoes from the past affecting you in the present, you can live each day fresh and new, without the risk of the past constantly coming through and blotting the unfolding living moment. Like this you can begin to be truly clear – clear of the past and clear in the present.

CLEANING YOUR SIDE OF THE STREET

The Dark Lists we've covered have included inventories of resentments, fears, dark secrets and an 'if only' list. But there's one more list that's required for you to be fully free and clear to step out of the past and into the next stage of your life without having to look over your shoulder. This list consists of everyone you think – or know – you've harmed in a big or small way, whether individuals or even organizations, and making amends wherever possible, if it is appropriate to do so.

Divide a blank page into three columns.

Take a few deep breaths and turn your attention to yourself and your past.

In the first column – and working forward in time – list all the people that in some way you feel you've harmed.

It can help if you work in five- or seven-year segments. Start with the first segment of your life, then move on to the next and so on, right up to the present day. If some of the harms you list aren't in the right sequence in terms of when they happened, don't worry. The important thing is that you do the work fearlessly, thoroughly and to the best of your ability from the very start. You'll be amazed at the profound effect that making this list will have once you've finished.

Cast your mind right back to the earliest memories you can access. Scanning these bite-sized chunks of your life, in the first column list all the people you've harmed. It might be someone you stole from, were violent to, let down or failed in some way, were unfaithful to, disloyal to, dishonest with or borrowed from without paying back.

Perhaps you were a gossip and spread malicious rumours, or made yourself feel superior at someone else's expense. Perhaps it was the things that you *didn't* do. Perhaps you weren't there when someone close to you needed you. Whatever the harm, if you can think of it, chances are it probably counts.

If you can still remember them, they need to be listed.

In the second column, and alongside your list of the names of people you've harmed, write down what it was that you did or didn't do.

In the third column, write down exactly how you'd feel if someone had done the same to you.

The purpose of this list is for you to start the process of making amends to the people listed on it. Just simply apologizing by saying 'sorry' will not suffice. Remember, actions speak louder than words. What's important is for you to show that you've changed.

Having made this list, what's important is being able to demonstrate that you've learned from your mistakes and that you're beginning to change the way you behave. You might need to make financial restitution. In my case, when I came in from the dark the list of financial damage was just so huge that I'm still in the process of making some of my last financial amends.

Sometimes repairing the damage that's been done can be a lifelong process.

The thing is having taken this on each day you'll be able to look life in the eye, honestly and honourably. You might not be able to sort out some of the things on your list overnight, but going through the process and beginning to acknowledge the wrongs that you've done will set you in the right direction to make amends over time. And because your past will no longer be haunting you beneath the surface of the present, you won't need to be looking over your shoulder all the time.

I recommend you make amends as soon as possible, otherwise sweet relationships might be lost forever. Once you've completed the list and understand and accept the harm done, start to implement whatever you need to do to address the damage. And remember, the point is that you're *willing* to do this. It may not be possible to do in each and every case but what's important is your willingness.

It's important you don't beat yourself up over the errors of your ways, or your sins of omission. The purpose of the list is simply to repair past harms – mostly those done to others but possibly also some to yourself.

The dark lists represent a bridge we're building. They'll lead you to freedom from your past – ready for your future in optimum shape.

There's another part to this exercise. It's really important you do it if you're going to be truly free of the past. It's a bit more challenging, but incredibly rewarding. I'll explain what it involves, but first I'd like to balance out The Dark Lists.

WRITING THE LIGHT LISTS

Because we're both dark and light, it's important to balance The Dark Lists with a list of all your positives. It's especially important to do this if you have a tendency to beat yourself up about things. If you are this way inclined, making The Dark Lists could send you nose-diving into a negative oblivion, so it's really important to balance The Dark Lists with a list of all your positives.

Again, you're going to need the A4 pad, exercise book or similar – just carry on using the one you've been using for your dark lists. It's a similar exercise but an affirmation and celebration of you – in the present.

Just as when you wrote your dark lists, find a place where you're not going to be disturbed and where you feel comfortable. Take your time and don't rush. Before starting the first list, take a few deep breaths and then turn your attention towards yourself once more.

On a blank page, write a list of all your inner assets and positive qualities. Perhaps imagine that you can see yourself through the eyes of a loved one. Focus on your best qualities and list these with conviction and strength – 'I am good at ...', 'I can ...' 'I am ...' – make each statement a positive.

The second list I'd like to suggest is of all the things that are currently in your life that you feel grateful for.

All the things that make you feel good about your life. This is a list you should make regularly.

The third list I'd recommend is of all the people, places and things that you really love. And if 'love' is too big a word for you here, then list what you really like.

First – all the people in your life that you love.

Second – all the places in your life that have meaning for you.

And third – all the things in your life that you appreciate and care about.

Once you've made your 'light lists', it would be a wonderful thing if you could share them with someone you're close to and cherish once you've completed all the exercises in this section. It would be wonderfully affirming for you to talk to someone you're close to about all the things you love and care about, and that make you enjoy being you. It would probably also mean a great deal to the person you choose to share this with.

It could be a way of bringing someone you're close to even closer. It'll help them get to know you better and show them what makes you tick positively. It may encourage them to do their own light lists and share them with you.

Remember, we're dealing with deep values and this is precious. Its essence is truth and love, and that's always good to share.

The light lists are your way of making the perceptual shift from feeling that your glass is half-empty to feeling that it's half-full. With constant practice, going back to your light lists and switching your glass back to half-full every time it feels like it's becoming half-empty, the shift will begin to take root. Regularly focusing on your positive qualities and assets, and being consciously grateful for them, is like watering that root with liquid nectar. It's called practising the 'attitude of gratitude'. I'm going to come back to this again later in the book.

THE VALUE OF SHARING YOUR DARK LISTS

Going through the process of voicing things that you feel ashamed of – or guilty and uncomfortable about – is a well-established practice on the spiritual path. It's been a central part of Christianity for centuries, and the value of talking about difficult issues is widely acknowledged.

Human beings are both dark and light, and it can be difficult enough to acknowledge our dark side, let alone talk about it. But bringing the shadowy aspects of our inner world into the light and acknowledging and facing these head-on can help turn our weaknesses into our strengths. Accepting aspects of yourself that you've tended to hide away can be truly transformative.

Accepting yourself as you are – both dark and light – has the power to set you free.

In order to be able to recover from the disease of addiction and alcoholism, I first had to acknowledge that I was both sick and completely beaten. By surrendering and giving up the fight – by throwing in the towel – I was able to quit and walk out of the arena as the real winner.

Accepting I was powerless over my addictions, and that my life was completely unmanageable, was my first step away from the battle. Owning up and admitting this to other people was another essential part of the process. Openly confessing the reality of my situation brought everything out into the open and enabled me to walk away a free man.

Sharing the darker details of your inner world can sometimes be a real challenge. Fear of being judged tends to be what makes us want to keep these kinds of things to ourselves, but that's just the ego – that self-obsessed part of our mind that spends its time worrying about what other people think. As the old country and western song goes, 'Your ego ain't your amigo.' This isn't about appearing 'good' or 'nice' in the eyes of others. This is about your long-term wellbeing. Believe it or not, ego-deflation is part of the 'cure'. Learning humility is a priceless key that opens the door to joining humanity on equal terms.

THE POWER OF VOICING YOUR DARK LISTS

Although the phrase 'a problem aired is a problem shared' might be a cliché, recognizing the value of doing just that was a crucial moment in my own recovery process.

By the time I got to the end of my path of self-destruction I was pretty much willing to go to any lengths to sort my life out. As I said before, desperation can actually be quite a gift. The thing is, we've always got choices. I was faced with the choice of doing something about my situation or going back to doing what I'd become sick and tired of doing.

Whether it's drink, drugs, food, shopping, cigarettes, sex, porn, gambling, being hypercritical of yourself and/or others, having a big gossiping mouth, being selfish or self-centred – whatever it is, choosing to do something about it and then sharing that decision with someone else creates an amazing chain reaction.

Having written all your lists, confessing those aspects of yourself that you may well feel ashamed of – your resentments, dark secrets, regrets and fears – will actually lighten your heavy load in a massive way. It's a really important part of the cleansing process.

It may seem a bit scary, but sharing all these things with another human being is a truly liberating experience.

VOICING THE DARK LISTS

The Dark Lists reflect elements of our negative internal baggage, stored in the subconscious, which have been 'secretly' influencing our external, conscious behaviour – influencing the way we are and shaping our reactions to external events and the choices we make. Each entry on your list will be particular and unique to you.

The fifth of the 12 steps involves admitting 'to God, ourselves and another human being the exact nature of our wrongs'. As I mentioned before, use your own concept of God – or a higher power – that works best for you. Having identified all your problems in the fourth step, the fifth involves admitting the precise nature of your wrongs to yourself, to another person, to the higher power – however you choose to define that – and to yourself. Once you've completed your dark lists, your next task is to find someone that you can trust to voice them to. You're not looking for comments or opinions, just someone you can trust who's a good listener.

Going through this part of the exercise will be of enormous benefit, and you really don't have to be as far down the road to perdition as I was to make it work for you.

It's a great thing to make these lists, but it's even greater releasing everything in them with your voice and getting them out into the fresh air. I can't stress how hugely beneficial it is to admit to the universe – God, yourself and another human being – the details of your dark lists.

It doesn't have to be someone you know, just someone who's willing to give you their time and ears as your 'witness'. Of course it could be a close friend or someone you feel is spiritually sound, or perhaps someone offering support on an appropriate helpline.

There are several places where you could do this incognito. The Samaritans offer an anonymous telephone service, and a priest will hear your confession whatever your religion, faith or belief and even if you're an agnostic or atheist.

Something miraculous happens when you go through this process. You'll begin to feel as though you've become joined to humanity – bonded by the imperfections, flaws and weaknesses we all share. It's this commonality of imperfection that levels and unites us; it challenges the ego's false assertions of flawlessness and superiority. Sharing this with another person acknowledges that, just like all the living things in this world, we are all perfectly imperfect.

In the 12-step programme, making your confession in a spiritual context, with God and another human being as your witness, is very important. However, if you're unable to find someone to listen to your lists, or you really don't feel comfortable doing this, then at least find a place where you'll be comfortable saying them alone, out loud: under a tree, by the sea or somewhere similar. You'll still find it an amazingly spiritually powerful thing to do. Perhaps you'll be able to find the right person later, when you're a little stronger and feel ready.

If it's possible, it would be good if you could share your lists with someone with a strong spiritual core, perhaps someone who's been through and understands the value of this process. Someone who's done the 12-step programme themselves would be an ideal witness.

You could try calling a 12-step telephone support line and explaining that you'd like to do the fifth step, and ask if there's anyone who'd be willing to act as your witness. The worst you can get is a 'No'. Don't be put off if this happens. However, if they've done the fifth step themselves, they just might be willing to hear you do yours. Even if you're not able to share your lists with another person – if all you can do is cast them privately to the sun, moon, stars or wind – it still means a lot and can be very powerful. Voicing the contents of your lists aloud acknowledges them not just to yourself but also to the 'power greater than you' and facilitates the process of release. Even expressing them aloud to Nature, being able to say, 'This is who I am, the best and the worst of me,' has enormous value. It's all part of becoming clear as you move towards the person you'd like to be.

As I've mentioned, drawing on the healing power of confession was a major milestone in my own recovery. Though it may seem a bit of a challenge, it's an invaluable component of this powerful method for purging the personality traits which, again and again, block us from enjoying truly being ourselves in the moment.

Ultimately, carrying around unresolved issues can take its toll on our physical bodies as well as on our minds and spirits. For example, you'd be right on the mark if you were to compare harbouring resentments to taking poison yourself in the hope that it would make someone else get sick and die.

It's time to give up the self-poisoning and move on.

3

THE PAST IS PAST – OR IS IT?

The great thing about the past is that it's now over. If this is how you feel, you're probably well and totally up to date with the 'baggage-management' of your past. If on the other hand you feel that things you're dealing with in the present are still being influenced by things that have happened to you in the past, you can't say it's over and done with yet. The past is not the past if it's still impinging on your present.

It's important to learn from the past – after all, you could say you're the sum total of everything you've been through. But if the negative effects of the past are influencing your decision-making, then the past is having a negative influence on the present.

If in the past you've been painfully rejected in a relationship by a man or woman and this now colours the way you are in your significant relationships, or even affects your wanting to pursue an intimate relationship, you're being limited by your past.

Sometimes I ask people to close their eyes and point to where they think their past is. If they point in front of them, chances are they're still seeing and reliving their past all the time.

It's really important to put the past behind us. Having said that, even if it's behind us but we keep looking at it in the rear view mirror, there's a danger we might be heading for an accident if our eyes aren't on the road ahead.

In order to be free of the negative past we need to deal with it, let go of it and give it its place – ideally behind us, in the past. To be our optimal selves we need to be able to look forward without worrying that the past is going to be replaying itself in the present.

To get the most from the present, we need to learn from the past, let go and move on.

BECOMING CLEAR

Becoming and being clear is about acknowledging your past and recognizing how it can affect everything in the present. If you can truly accept and understand the past, it's likely you're no longer going to be letting accumulated baggage influence and limit your present.

Becoming and being clear is about living in the moment. Rather than bringing the past with you into the present, being clear is about taking each moment as it comes and taking each person you meet as they come.

Becoming and being clear comes about when the past no longer has such a profound influence on how you are in the present – when you've acknowledged the negative past and put a stop to it shaping and influencing you in the present.

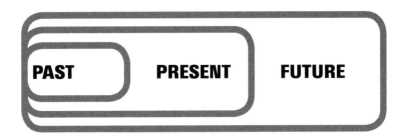

STEPPING INTO THE NEW STORY

Leaving the past behind involves stepping out of your old story and stepping into the story you've chosen for yourself. The old story has actually served you well in that it's got you this far to the point where you're ready to change.

To prepare to step into your new story take a moment to imagine the person you'd really like to be. Imagine what it is you'd really like to achieve in this short life. Imagining your new journey unfolding ahead of you is a great way of beginning.

Life is all about the journey. Make it a journey towards what you want to be doing and who you want to be. Step into your new story with an idea of the sort of person you aspire or dream to be and start moving towards that dream today and be the best you can, one day at a time.

You're going to have to let go of the map you've been using until now and go off-piste. Your journey's going to combine your dreams and your discovery of what the universe – or higher power – has scripted for you. Wherever the old story came from, if it's no longer really working for you, let it go.

More than likely there's another story waiting for you to step into that's far greater and more fulfilling than the one you've been telling yourself up till now.

> '*Success is not the key to happiness. Happiness is the key to success. If you love what you are doing, you will be successful.*'
>
> HERMAN CAIN

Before I abandoned my old script, I never imagined I'd be doing what I'm doing now. Through a series of disasters, frustrations and rather serious mishaps I realized that the map I was following, and my ideas about life, no longer had any relevance. Lost and confused during the early part of my recovery, I started to realize there was a very different journey waiting for me.

When I finally let go and opened myself up to this possibility, it paved the way for some quite extraordinary coincidences. One by one, and sometimes within the space of a few days, a succession of answers was revealed that have led me to where I am now, including writing this for you.

Our past can prevent us from finding our true purpose and journey. Help yourself to release your negative past and you'll become primed for your new story, which is just waiting to unfold when you're clear and ready.

THE IMPORTANCE OF REGULAR RENEWAL

Renewal is a clearing and cleansing process. It involves clearing out all the internal baggage – or for some of us, clearing actual wreckage from the past – to enable us to stand in the light of the present. And because the present is in a state of dynamic change, ongoing renewal is vital. Renewal enables us to avoid getting stuck and to be the best we can be in each and every moment – creating both a better, baggage-free present and future.

Sometimes when we're in the process of clearing the past – living presently and working at being the best we can be in each moment – self-neglect can still creep back in. It's really important to remember that *old habits die hard*. As I said in the Introduction to this book, self-help has to be an ongoing process.

To avoid getting caught up in old and unhelpful beliefs, patterns and habits, we need to develop an ongoing, honest self-appraisal. It's important to keep checking and double-checking that we haven't distorted what's actually happening from moment to moment based on our old ways of thinking and interpreting the world. We need to take stock to make sure that how we're interpreting what's happening is actually what's happening, particularly at times when we're feeling unsettled or insecure.

The process of renewal gives us the clarity to meet each moment truly as it is, and the ability to live life on life's terms in each moment without slipping into distorted thinking, even when the present feels particularly uncomfortable. Accepting the challenge of adversity as being what we're *meant* to be going through is a positive way of aligning ourselves with the present and navigating our way through it, rather than thinking we're being persecuted or part of some sort of huge cosmic mistake.

Renewal enables us to recommit to physical, spiritual and mental wellbeing, and align ourselves with the universe's plan for us. It helps us avoid getting caught up with feelings of frustration and discord about whatever's happening in the moment, and thinking that what is isn't meant to be what is.

'As we move through the moment, wherever we are now is where we're meant to be.'

ECKHART TOLLE

OUR RIGHT DIRECTION

I remember going to see the band U2 in the mid-1980s and somehow miraculously finding myself in a conversation with Bono after the gig. We ended up talking well into the early hours of the morning at the hotel the band was staying in. What particularly stood out for me from that long and deep discussion – in which we touched on all points of the spiritual compass – was the fact that Bono didn't believe in coincidences. He called them 'Godincidences', and used this word to describe the wonderful happenings that miraculously appear in our lives.

We were both able to recognize these 'miracles' playing their part in shaping the course of our lives. Although I needed to lose the path on my own journey a few years after that meeting, our conversation made me notice and acknowledge the extraordinary coincidences that seemed like more than just 'luck' whenever they happened. Now I always make sure I say 'thank you' for these miracles, or special moments, whenever they appear in my life.

Look out for them in your own life; they are like little signs sent to guide you. Interpret them as you wish, but keep an open mind.

I'm not yet enlightened enough to know how the universe works and whether or not things do happen for a reason, but I feel far better in myself when I'm thinking positively and am open to the possibility.

One way or another we're all on this extraordinary and wonderful journey called life. Where we're going seems to be partially up to us and partially up to what happens to us and around us. How we cope with it all, and how we process and navigate our way through it is essentially the great challenge we all face.

Getting on the path, ditching the baggage of the past and continually reappraising the situation in the present in order to keep on the path is fundamental to where I'm at now. It's been the foundation of my own Self help process.

Releasing the negative past has cleared the way for an unfolding, ever-expanding map that's colouring itself in as I go. Compared to where I was before I got on this path the runway lights for my new life are now on.

PART 2

THE RULES OF
THE MIND

The next part of this book is devoted to what I call the 'mechanics of the mind'. It's an attempt to reduce the seemingly abstract workings of the mind to rules we can understand and then use to our advantage to help us on our journey.

When you're learning to drive you need to get to know the rules of the road. Unless you're familiar with the Highway Code you're going to cause accidents and you're never going to pass your test. Similarly, when you're on the path we're treading in this book, understanding these rules of the mind will help you negotiate the route, deal with the road's twists and turns, and avoid oncoming traffic.

Sometimes, despite our seemingly best efforts, we can find ourselves baffled by limitation. Understanding the rules I outline in this section will help you develop strategies that'll support you to progress, achieve and even exceed your goals and enjoy success.

When I was young I remember wishing that I could have a guidebook for my life – something that would provide me with a manual for living – but I just never came across the right one. Now that I'm a fully fledged, grown-up adult – and having survived so many different catastrophes – I've got a far better idea of the path, what to watch out for to stay on it, what to do and what not to do.

The rules I outline are worth remembering. Hopefully they'll help you negotiate your path a little better, though they're neither definitive nor without exception.

EVERY THOUGHT HAS A PHYSICAL REACTION

Understanding and accepting that everything you think about produces a physical effect or reaction can be immediately liberating. As soon as you acknowledge and accept this rule, you're naturally going to want to manage what you think about in order to produce the physical effects you'd like to experience.

Taking place in your mind, thoughts are the things you tell yourself about what you're experiencing. They're like filters for your opinions and your particular take on what's happening in the present, what you imagine lies ahead in the myriad possibilities for your future and what you think may be coming next. These filters are subject to change, depending on how you're thinking.

If you imagine that you're walking down a dark alley at night on the wrong side of town, hearing the sound of bottles breaking and footsteps coming from behind you, you'll probably be able to make yourself feel quite uneasy. You'll probably want to imagine walking a little faster and you'll feel your heart rate increasing.

Now imagine that you're walking on a sandy shore, looking at a blue sea, with the sounds of the breeze in the palm trees. You'll probably be able to bring about calm, warm and relaxed feelings.

Both of these imagined scenarios are thoughts, and produce opposite physical reactions caused by the chemicals released by your brain and nervous system in response to those thoughts.

In your day-to-day life if you imagine things going wrong you'll probably start feeling bad even before anything actually goes wrong. You're creating a physiological response to a thought. By understanding this principle you can become consciously empowered to begin to *choose* what thoughts you might want to think about, either positive or negative. Every thought, whether it's imagined or based in reality, will have an effect in the physical dimension.

Essentially, feelings and emotions are the end results of our thoughts. Some are pleasant and some not so pleasant. Worry, grief, anger, anxiety, fear and depression can all have an impact on the body in a detrimental way. Of course, there's often no way of avoiding these feelings. What's important is that they're acknowledged and then let go, not held onto.

When you notice a negative feeling, follow it back to the thought that caused it – and choose well what you dwell on.

With practice it is possible to learn to 'thought-stop' those thoughts that can have a potentially negative physical impact, and replace them with more positive thoughts. Not so easy to do with the stronger thoughts that cause stronger emotions, but still possible with practice. In Part Three I'm going to introduce you to a technique I call Breathing Plus. It's very effective for snapping out of negative thinking.

Rather than having your mind chatter away on autopilot in the background, become more aware of what you're thinking. Notice whether your thoughts are inclined towards the positive or the negative. Noticing this will give you the option to thought-stop – and thought-*switch* to the opposite.

It's unlikely you're going to want to spend time on thoughts that make you feel bad. Positive thinking optimizes your physical state and puts you in a far better physiological condition to deal with life's ups and downs. Learning to choose your mind's subject matter will have remarkable effects on your inner condition, your health and on the way you feel.

IMAGINATION IS POWERFUL

'Imagination is everything. It is the preview of life's coming attractions.'

ALBERT EINSTEIN

Your imagination is a very powerful tool. Far stronger than the conscious mind, it can set you up to fail or to succeed. The process of using your imagination allows you to visualize your dreams and rehearse achieving them. When you imagine something you can actually fool the subconscious into thinking that it's a reality.

Sigmund Freud, the father of psychoanalysis, described the mind as an iceberg. He argued that less than 10 per cent of its content floats above the surface of consciousness. Freud believed that the bulk of the mind's content lies beneath conscious thought and that most of it is contained in the unconscious. The imagination acts like a conduit for the unconscious and, in its ability to undermine rational thought, can have more power to convince than actual fact.

Vertigo (or the fear of heights) is a good example. When faced with a long drop, or the idea of a long drop, people who suffer from vertigo imagine they're going to fall. Even when there's a safety barrier separating them from the drop, they may well experience the sensations of vertigo. The sensations they feel are as a result of the power of their imagination. They're not going to fall, but they imagine they will.

Worry can create pictures of things we're fearful of happening, to the extent that the subconscious mind believes that they're *actually* happening.

Shakespeare's *Othello* provides another great example of the power of the imagination. In the play, the wicked Iago feeds Othello's jealous imagination to the point that he actually believes his wife Desdemona has been unfaithful, even though they love each other and there's no conclusive evidence to suggest that she has cheated on him.

Jealousy is a good example of the way in which the imagination can produce mental images that override reason and become the blueprint for limiting and potentially destructive patterns of reactive behaviour. With this in mind, it's crucial that we're aware of our thoughts and able to differentiate between what's real and what's imagined.

Of course, the imagination can also be a great source for supporting success through positive inspiration. Sports psychologists understand the power and value of the imagination and use it in mental rehearsal to create the ideal physiological conditions for athletes to achieve positive outcomes, targets and winning results.

Later on in the book I'm going to give you an exercise that'll show you how you can use your imagination to achieve your goals.

4

YOU CAN'T HAVE TWO OPPOSING THOUGHTS

'The mind is the most capricious of insects –
flitting, fluttering.'

Virginia Woolf

Buddhists compare the mind to a monkey moving though the branches of a tree because of the way it jumps from thought to thought. Unless it's brought under control, the mind does indeed tend to behave like a monkey or insect.

Though you can move from one thought or feeling to another pretty quickly, you can't experience two opposing emotions, or even two opposing thoughts, at the same time. This is very fortunate – the workings of the mind can be confusing enough as it is and that would be just too much.

The good news is, you don't have to put up with the thoughts and feelings that your mind throws at you. You can learn to change them for thoughts and feelings you'd rather have, thoughts that make you feel good. It's really important to choose what you think about, because the mind magnifies whatever it focuses on.

It is possible to, quite literally, change our minds. Anxiety and negative thinking can spiral into depression or destructive behaviour – in my case, self-medication – so it's important to get off that train as soon as you notice you're on it. Again, this is why it's essential to be aware, or 'mindful', of what you're thinking.

You've probably met people who always seem to be complaining about one thing or another. Some people are like that – constantly focusing on the negatives, and most probably only ever able to see obstacles and never opportunities. You may have a tendency to be like this yourself. If you are, it's time to change your mind, because thinking like this is stopping you from making the most of your life. It doesn't matter how tough your circumstances are, you can choose to shift your perspective.

Squashed into a cramped and airless room with several other people, hiding from Hutu death squads during the Rwandan genocide, Immaculee Ilibagiza survived her ordeal mentally intact – unlike the others with her – by focusing her thoughts on the power of love and prayer. There are lots of examples of people who've gone through horribly exacting trials and survived, by remaining positively focused.

Learn to use PMA – a 'Positive Mental Attitude'.

If you find yourself thinking about things that make you feel less than good, shift your train of thought to things that make you feel positive – like being successful, things you enjoy doing, happy memories, people you like, things you're looking forward to doing. With practice you'll find it easier to switch and, if you have a tendency towards negative thinking, to stay switched for longer and longer.

THE LAW OF ATTRACTION

*'All that we are is a result of
what we have thought.'*

BUDDHA

The more you think about something the more you will it into existence, so be careful what you think about. If you dwell on your fears it'll be difficult for you to move beyond them and you run the risk of drawing to yourself the things you least want in your life.

The life, people and things you attract to yourself will always reflect your inner being.

WHAT YOU THINK ABOUT YOU GET MORE OF

'What you resist persists.'

CARL JUNG

When you try *not* to think about something, it actually sticks it to you. Try not to think about the colour yellow and it'll attach you even more to that colour. To dis-attach, think of something else. If you constantly think and worry about not being poor and not being a failure, even though you really want to be rich, there's a danger you may end up being a poor failure.

If you focus on what you *don't* want, don't be surprised if that's what you get.

Spend more time thinking about what you really want, not what you're afraid of.

63

If you want something badly enough and think about it a lot, like being drawn by a magnet you'll find yourself heading towards it. The key is to be able to enjoy what you've got and also where you are on your journey.

YOU ARE WHAT YOU THINK

'What you think you become.'

Buddha

Increase your belief in yourself and your expectations for yourself and you will increase your potential. Whatever you think about yourself, you become. We impose and reflect our own limits on ourselves and our lives.

Observe your thoughts and start to develop a sense of what you tend to think about and the way you tend to think, because the way you think shapes the person you are and the life you expect to live.

We have a choice about how we are on the inside and about the thoughts that we allow to occupy our minds. Ask yourself if you want to indulge your resentful, negative, downtrodden victim-self or would rather find and be your best self.

If you're anything like I used to be, you may notice a lot of your thinking revolves around comparing yourself to others. If you have a tendency to do this, bear in mind the saying – 'compare and despair'.

Beware, poisonous thoughts poison their owner, so don't let that negative inner voice get the upper hand. Learn to bring the focus of your thoughts back to self-care and self-acceptance – always strive to be your best. Remember, no one can be YOU better than you can.

Notice your thoughts, become mindful and start to believe you can be the person you want to be.

What you think about you become, and as you believe so shall you be.

WHAT THE MIND BELIEVES THE BODY ACHIEVES

'Change your thinking, change your life.'
Ernest Holmes

If a mental condition lasts long enough it will bring about a physical change. The longer an idea remains in the mind, the more fixed it becomes and the more it will condition your behaviour.

Using mental rehearsal to imagine what you can do becomes the instruction for your body to prepare to do it. Believing in a possibility creates the potential for your achieving it.

As you believe, so shall it be.

'If you're going to think anyway, think big!'
Donald Trump

PART 3

CREATING THE CONDITIONS FOR THE OPTIMAL YOU

'You can be a guiding star if you make the most of who you are.'

AUTHOR UNKNOWN

When I was in rehab, a nurse left a card with this quote on my pillow. I've used it as a grid reference ever since. It resonated with me at the time and now it reminds me of where I was. It's one of the mantras I use to keep me focused on where I'm aiming for.

In Part One I talked about the effects the past can have on us and how these can hinder us from enjoying the life we'd like to be living. In Part Three, I'm going to take things a stage further and look at how you can start being the person you'd like to be and keep moving towards where you're aiming for.

5

'MOREISM' – THE ENDLESS SEARCH FOR ENOUGH

When I was about seven years old I remember my father in a state of total frustration saying to me 'Nothing ever seems to be enough for you – you always want more!' And he was right. For many years I was driven by a part of me that was always hungry and that was never at peace, except when I acquired something new and managed to get a bit of short-term pleasure and relief.

Before I started to turn my life around I was dogged by an almost constant feeling that I needed to obtain things. As a teenager I built up a huge collection of comics. I was also obsessional about Frisbee and skateboarding. I applied my compulsive-addictive behaviour to both and was driven to be the best and to get as many awards and accolades as I could. Later on it became all about buying the latest cool things.

Whether I was consuming, achieving, taking or winning, I always had this sense that I needed more. Deep down I felt that somehow what I had was not enough. Whatever I got was never sufficient to satisfy that undercurrent of 'want'.

The sense of satisfaction from having something new never seemed to last. It just led me to feeling like I needed more new things. I felt literally driven by this constant desire for more, and nothing was ever enough to fix it. Back then I wasn't interested in trying to understand why I felt like I did, but now I know it's not uncommon. Since sorting myself out I've met so many people who are driven by the same kind of unquenchable craving.

Perhaps there's an aspect of it that's positive and even evolutionary in terms of our wanting to 'improve' ourselves and our life's situation. But, fed by the seductive images of the consumerist society, this can easily become superficial and surface, and usually limited to the materialistic. I call it the disease of 'Moreism', and it's incredibly contagious.

I've heard many old-timers in 12-step meetings talk about the 'ism' of alcoholism as standing for 'I-self-me'. This definition works really well in the context of 'Moreism'. It's a condition that locks our perception into a cul-de-sac of surface self-appraisal, and pushes us towards measuring who we are and how we feel in relation to what we have.

Moreism is all about us endlessly trying to make ourselves feel better from the outside when we feel uncomfortable on the inside. It's about us trying to make ourselves feel more complete when, deep down, we feel something's missing.

In the past I used to try to make myself feel better with anything from sweets, chocolate and food to a new pair of shoes, clothes, endless CDs, alcohol and drugs. I was always looking for something outside myself in an attempt to resolve issues going on inside. The things I tried to do this with were all immediately satisfying in one way or another, but totally short-term. I was an insatiable Moreist, caught up in looking for an 'outside solution to an inside problem'.

When I was buying things I always felt good, but often on the way home the uneasy feelings would start up again. I identify Moreism as being at the root of shopping addiction. Moreism is tied into a mindset that's been described as the need for 'the external validation of self'. This way of thinking is underpinned by the distorted belief that who or what we are is based on what we've got and how we look.

Until the situation inside is transformed, from feeling that something is lacking to a feeling that we are whole and complete as we are, external fixes to internal issues are only ever going to be temporary. Unless the internal issue is sorted out, all the external things we acquire merely create the temporary illusion of being complete. The feeling of emptiness or dis-ease will always creep back, leading us to continue to be Moreistic.

The psychologist Oliver James has coined the phrase 'affluenza' to describe the ways we're conditioned by what he calls 'selfish capitalism' to focus on the satisfaction of external 'needs'. In his view, being encouraged to think we *need* to have a 'better' car, the latest gadgets, fashionable clothes or more 'desirable' accessories to 'improve' our lives is like a sickness. Its effect is ever-increasing levels of unhappiness.

Moreism is a symptom of an interior negative self-perception. It's caused by a feeling that there's a vacuum inside, and that nothing within us has any real value or relevance. With our attention perpetually tuned to the external fix, we have no real sense of our interior dimension beyond niggling worries and anxieties: the resentments, fears and regrets that bubble to the surface. We need to look deeper within, beyond these distortions.

EGO = EASING GOD OUT

At its root, this endless desire for more things is fuelled by our ego's need to keep up with and feel better than other people. As I said in Part One, the ego is that self-obsessed part of the mind that spends its time revolving around its own closed orbit of empty self-interest.

There's an acronym for the ego that sums it up: 'Easing God Out'. Even though it might do its best to pretend to be God, the ego's nothing like 'the power greater than our normal selves'.

We've all got an ego, but if we give it too much attention it's going to have us thinking all sorts of nonsense about being superior to the rest of the world. It'll keep us locked up in our heads being narcissistic and comparing ourselves to other people, getting bogged down in the past and tied up with worrying about the future. Setting itself up as God, the ego separates us from having a conscious connection with something infinite and beyond our understanding. I remember being told by a long-time recovered member of AA – 'There's only one thing you need to know about the power greater than you and that is, YOU are not it!'

Too many of us spend too much time living in our heads feeding the insecure ego and its need to feel 'better than'. Exclusively attaching ourselves to it limits us to a two-dimensional, surface-level, often fear-based kind of existence. If we base our self-perception on the mental and physical dimensions alone, something will always be missing.

YOU ARE MORE THAN YOUR EGO

It's likely that if we limit ourselves to existing in two dimensions then we're going to have a hard time achieving a sense of deep and permanent fulfilment. And it's probable that we'll get caught up in the physical dimension in a constant and fruitless search for something that seems to be missing. I know I spent a lot of time doing that.

To be able to combat the disease of Moreism it's vital that we make an inner shift and challenge our ego's attempts to control and dominate the way we think about ourselves and the world around us. It's important for our total health and wellbeing that we begin to think about life in three, rather than just two dimensions.

The three dimensions I'm referring to are the mental, physical *and* spiritual. Recognizing and becoming conscious of all three has helped me start enjoying simply being in the present, without the feeling that I need to add anything to myself. It's helped me feel that, in each moment, I'm enough as I am.

There seem to be three key questions underlying life – Who am I? Why am I here? What happens when I die? These questions reflect the three dimensions of the mental, physical and spiritual.

ACCEPTING THE CIRCLE OF LIFE

Acknowledging we have an end can be an uncomfortable thought, particularly if we've been brought up in a culture that tends to brush the idea of death and dying under the carpet.

Unlike the culture in which I was brought up, Buddhist belief systems accept pain and suffering as fundamental aspects of being alive and human. Accepting that life includes pain, suffering and sadness makes it easier for me to embrace the challenges of adversity. It's made me more battle-ready because, let's face it, life is difficult and can be a bit of a battle at times.

> *'Pain is inevitable but misery is optional. We cannot avoid pain but we can avoid joy.'*
>
> TIM HANSEL

I've had clients who have talked to me about their inability to see a point to life because of the inevitability of death. They've told me that they've spent most of their lives in total fear of the fact that they are going to die.

It's a core issue that each one of us has to deal with. We can try to ignore it, deny it or convince ourselves that we're immortal, but it'll never go away. The fact that none of us is going to be here forever, and that nobody knows empirically what happens to our consciousness after we've gone, are issues that underscore human life.

These are issues that are profoundly disturbing to the ego, and for some people a source of serious trauma. I remember lying in my bed at an early age and often getting into a state of fear and anxiety, realizing that I wasn't going to be here for very long and that I was going to die.

It gave me an undercurrent sense of panic that I felt most acutely when I was lying in bed alone at night. Then one night, after many years of this, in a moment of quiet I heard a voice inside me saying 'Max, everybody dies, do not be afraid, it's normal.' It was an incredible moment and brought about a profound realization. As I thought about it I felt a great sense of comfort. I felt that, just as I had been somewhere before I was born, the thought of returning back there when I died didn't seem so disturbing any more. And I was comforted by the knowledge that it's not just me. We all die, it's normal. This is the circle of life.

Having come so close to the actual experience during my drug-induced, near-death moments, I've realized that what really matters is the extraordinariness of being at all. Spending time looking for answers to an unanswerable question is focusing on the wrong thing.

Carpe diem – seize the day: life is for living!

I now think that having the chance to exist at all is the most remarkable thing. To have a body that lives and breathes, that functions as best it can despite the things that happen to it and that it gets put through, to be able to create and adapt to our individual and collective circumstances and environments in the diverse ways in which we do, is the real wonder.

Experiencing myself beyond my ego and embracing the fact that life can have a spiritual dimension hasn't given me all the answers. In fact, it's led to more questions. But acknowledging the three dimensions has made it a lot easier to enjoy simply being in the here and now and to develop the capacity to find myself smiling more often, for no obvious or particular reason. I'm learning not to take myself so seriously.

THE ANTIDOTE TO 'MOREISM'

The modern-day spiritual teacher Eckhart Tolle encourages us to find 'the extraordinary in the ordinary' and over 200 years ago William Blake wrote about seeing 'a world in a grain of sand, and a heaven in a wild flower'.

Throughout time people have recognized the magic and wonder of being alive, and also the fact that being alive is only ever experienced in the fleeting instant of the present moment. When I was caught up in the dis-ease of Moreism, I rarely spent any time appreciating being in the here and now. By constantly looking outside myself and thinking about what I wanted to acquire, I was killing each moment and literally wasting my precious time.

Hitting mental, physical and spiritual rock-bottom and going into recovery forced me to re-appraise my life and how I'd been living it up to that point. Following through with the process of releasing my negative past enabled me to face up to how I'd been living in a way that prevented me from 'being' in the present.

As I began to move beyond the need to experience myself through the haze of drugs and the things I acquired, I slowly started to be able to feel more and more comfortable with being present in the here and now. I started to discover what it's like to feel truly alive and to experience the 'now'. I was actually able to see, hear and feel what it is to exist in the moment.

A backlog of unresolved fears, resentments, doubts and distortions can often lie just beneath the surface of our conscious minds like unwanted furniture slung into a canal. All that wreckage needs to be dredged out and thrown onto a huge bonfire of purification.

To become truly clear, to enjoy living presently and in the 'now', requires clearing our negative past and acknowledging, challenging and addressing our self-limiting beliefs, negative perceptions and distortions. All of these fuel Moreism if they're unresolved.

As I mentioned in Part One, the first step of the 12 steps involves admitting that you've got a problem which your 'normal' self can't seem to solve.

The second step involves opening yourself to the spiritual concept of a power greater than you – whatever that might mean for you personally – that can help you to solve your problem and restore you to sanity.

The third step involves asking that power to take care of you and help you make the changes you need to make in order to turn your life around.

The fourth step involves fearlessly making a thorough inventory in order to release yourself from the negative past – the lists of all those things that stop you from enjoying your true Self, which we covered in Part One.

In the next chapter I'm going to introduce you to a few more very straightforward exercises that have helped me on my path to recovery and given me tools with which to address issues that were clouding my own ability to experience the joy of living.

6

PRACTISING SELF-CARE

It's up to you to decide what your vision for the optimum you is, but I'd encourage you to think of it in relation to the three dimensions I mentioned in the last chapter: the mental, physical and spiritual.

I believe our true, optimal self depends on these three areas being balanced and maintained in a state of wellness and health – and we ignore this at our peril!

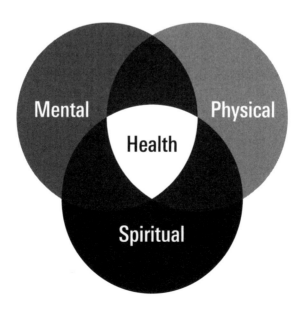

MENTAL WELLNESS

Mental wellness is crucial. It's underpinned by a feeling of being balanced and untroubled by unresolved issues and negative emotions, like fear and guilt. Mental wellbeing is all about being able to transcend.

It includes acknowledging that you may not have solved all the issues you might want to but that you're dealing with things as best you can in the present time, and not giving yourself a hard time because you're not yet where you want to be and still a work in progress.

Mental wellness involves recognizing that being on the journey is itself the Holy Grail.

PHYSICAL WELLNESS

Physical wellness is a relative state, but wherever we might be on the health spectrum it's really important to stay attentive to the body's signals of wellbeing and to be able to listen to what your body is telling you about the way it's feeling in the present: ensuring it's adequately nourished by a balanced and healthy diet, rested by sleep, maintained by some kind of regular physical exercise and oxygenated to its optimum by the habitual practice of full breathing – which I'll introduce to you in the next few pages.

Breathing in ways that enhance consciousness is fundamental to both physical and mental wellness. It enables us to stay attentive and underpins our ability to transcend.

SPIRITUAL WELLNESS

Spiritual wellness keeps us connected to the connection that's always there, helps us get beyond the shallow two-dimensional ego-state and affirms a real sense of the priceless nature of all living things. Giving time for the contemplation of Nature can really help with your ability to connect with the spiritual and the Infinite. It puts everything into a different kind of perspective to the one that's limited by focusing only on yourself.

THE 'ALL ABOUT ME' SHOW

Connecting with a spiritual dimension within, and acknowledging this dimension at play in all things, presses the 'pause' button on the remote that broadcasts the 'all about me' show as an ongoing loop.

Starting from a really young age we can quickly get into the habit of being limited to considering the world around us in relation to how it affects 'me, myself and I'.

If we're fortunate enough to have had loving and attentive parents, chances are they're initially going to have made us feel like the centre of their world. Thinking the world revolves around our own self-centred needs and wants can be a difficult habit to break out of. It's called growing up. Sometimes people who look like adults still have a lot of growing up to do. I know because I was one of them. It can also make us very susceptible to manipulation by anyone who can pull the strings of our selfish vanities (think advertisers for starters), so it's a habit well worth breaking.

THE 'PLASTIC' BRAIN

Getting into behavioural habits is all part of being human, so it's in our best interest to make sure that the habits we get into are going to contribute to our becoming the optimal being we're working towards.

There's a reason why we find it so easy to slip into repeated patterns of behaviour. Our brains are like a hugely complex junction box, but instead of wires and fuses they're comprised of neurons and glial cells. The role of the neurons is to transmit impulses and messages around the brain, and relay them to the rest of the body, while the glial cells provide support by maintaining the brain's environment.

You could also compare the brain to an extraordinarily complex computer, but unlike a Mac or PC it's totally organic. There are no circuit boards, drives or processors, just lots of cells (neurons and glia), water and neurotransmitters ('nerve chemicals').

In the past, scientists thought that by the time we reached adulthood our brains were pretty much set but some neuroscientists are now suggesting otherwise. Rather than being fixed, the brain seems to have an intelligent 'plasticity' that enables us to learn, adapt and develop throughout our lives.

The brain's neural pathways – along which information, commands and impulses are transmitted – seem to be able to realign and reconfigure themselves in relation to new stimuli they're exposed to. Each time we do something new, we open up the possibility for the configuration of a new neural pathway.

Even as adults we have literally billions of unused brain cells ready and waiting to become active. New ideas and experiences, patterns of thought and behaviours, can become established as neural pathways. The more the behaviour is practised, or ideas engaged with, the stronger the pathways become. And if continued, over time the well-beaten track becomes a road and over even more time, as the behaviour becomes habituated, the neural pathway becomes a superhighway. It's important to do new things or to do old things differently, or to think in new ways to keep the mind more fluid, open and adaptive.

CHANGING STATE TO CHANGE DIRECTION

During my recovery, and as I was putting myself back together, I discovered a system that utilizes the brain's plasticity to bring about sustained personal change. Neuro-Linguistic Programming (NLP) was first developed in the US in the early 1970s by Richard Bandler and John Grinder.

NLP is both an art and a science. It's based on the idea that the way we translate sensory information into thoughts and ideas affects our internal state, physiology and behaviour. It's not so much the information but the way we interpret and process that information that determines the effect it has on us.

This in turn has an impact on the way we engage and interact with the world, and on the outcomes of our interactions and engagement with it. The way we process information and experience, and the way that affects us as individuals, shape the way we conduct our lives and communicate and interact with the people in it.

NLP techniques can help us look at the ideas we have about ourselves and others, the kinds of words and phrases we habitually use to describe the model of the world we perceive we're living in. By developing an awareness of these things in ourselves, and beginning to recognize them in other people, NLP enables us to change and adapt the way we tend to communicate and think about the world around us for the better. By practising its techniques it's possible to change a negative world-view into a positive one.

NLP is based on the assumption that we can actually change how we feel about ourselves and the world relatively quickly. One of the many methods it uses to do this is through 'state-changing' techniques. These techniques help us to develop pathways in the brain which, when activated, take us straight into a positive state of mind.

ANCHORING 'TRIGGER POINTS'

One of these techniques involves the use of physical 'trigger points' which have become linked to positive feelings or experiences through a process called 'anchoring'. Essentially, the selected trigger point – or points – connect to neural pathways in the brain which, when activated, can generate a desired state. Triggering the anchored connection brings about a dramatic shift in our immediate mental, emotional and physical state whenever a shift is required.

By making a physical association between a particular body part and a particular feeling (e.g. confidence, resourcefulness, contentedness, courage, creativity), through a mental association between that body part and a memory of that feeling or positive experience, trigger points can quickly take us from feeling bad to feeling good.

I regularly use this technique in my one-to-one sessions with clients, and it's also something you can learn to do for yourself. The way I introduce it is to get the person I'm working with to remember and think about three or four positive memories.

I then get them to find and choose their trigger point. This might be the tip of the thumb and the forefinger joined together, squeezing an ear lobe in a special way, pressing their tongue against a particular point inside their mouth or straightening up and lifting the vertebra of the spine – basically, stimulating whatever place or part of their body they wish to use as their trigger point.

In order to anchor a positive feeling to the trigger point they've chosen, I ask them to close their eyes, draw in a breath and then, as they exhale, to remember a time when they felt really, really, good. When they have a particular memory in mind, I ask them to nod their head or say 'yes'.

Then I get them to go into the memory as though they're really there again reliving it in their body, seeing exactly what they saw, hearing the sounds they could hear, and even feeling the feelings they felt. I ask them to recall the memory in such vivid detail to the extent that they feel as if they're actually really there. At this point I'll ask them to make the memory even more real – to imagine it brighter, clearer and richer – and the feelings even stronger and completely vivid all around them.

At the memory's absolute peak I ask them to anchor the associated feelings using the pre-chosen trigger point – by squeezing their thumb and forefinger or ear lobe, by pressing their tongue against the special place inside their mouth or wherever they've chosen.

Then I'll get them to 'break state', usually by opening their eyes and looking around the room for a moment, or to focus elsewhere by thinking about something else.

We'll repeat this exercise at least two or three more times, recalling other positive memories. I may get them to call up a memory of a moment in which they felt extremely confident, another in which they felt very strong and resilient, and perhaps one in which they felt inspired or creative.

Perhaps I'll ask them to remember a time when they were with other people and feeling particularly good – a positive memory about being on excellent form with others around them, or alone in a natural environment, by the sea or amongst trees, feeling a deep sense of clarity and connectedness.

Whatever positive memories we both agree would make the ideal blend of feelings to improve things, they learn to generate those feelings again whenever they want to change their internal state from being less than great to feeling excellent.

'STACKING' ANCHORS

I'd like to introduce you to a special breathing exercise I use for 'stacking' anchored connections. It involves layering a series of positive anchors – one on top of another – and linking them to a single 'trigger point' that harnesses the power of your breath. The exercise provides groundwork preparation for a technique I call Breathing Plus. Breathing Plus is the process of being able to make your breath MORE than just your 'normal' breath. It involves fully stretching your lungs to their maximum capacity and using this point as the trigger of a positive inner switch.

When you begin, I'm going to ask you to remember a series of highly positive memories, one by one. I'm going to explain how you can then anchor them, one at a time, to the same trigger point – the point at which your lungs are stretched to their maximum capacity. The exercise is in four parts, and I'd recommend you do it sitting down.

Part 1

To begin with I want you to take a slow deep breath and at the same time close your eyes for a moment. Then as you exhale, reach into your mind and find a positive memory of a time when you thought to yourself – 'I feel great.' Think of a time when you remember feeling REALLY good.

Maybe you were on holiday, walking on a beach in the summertime, in a field or by a river, laughing, or even dancing to your favourite record – or some other special moment when you remember thinking to yourself, 'I'm feeling really great!'

When you've found the memory, I want you to go back into it as though you're there again, right now; seeing what you saw, feeling what you felt and even hearing what you heard. You can TURN UP the colour and the brightness to make the memory even more 'real' – so that you feel you're right back there again.

While you're there, take another deep breath – right up to the fullest stretch of your lungs and hold it for few moments … before exhaling. Then open your eyes to break the state.

Part 2

Now, to layer your second positive memory onto the first, take another slow deep breath and at the same time close your eyes for a moment. As you exhale, reach into your mind again and find a positive memory that involves you feeling good interacting with others around you.

It could either be a social or a business situation in which the people you're with are probably enjoying your company too but we're only interested in the fact that you're enjoying yourself and feeling really good interacting with them.

When you've found that memory, I want you to go back into it again and to feel that you're really with those people – right now. See them in front of you, feel what you felt – really enjoying the way you're being with them.

As you did before, TURN UP the colour and the brightness – make the memory even more 'real'. And take a deep breath, right up to the fullest stretch of your lungs; hold it for a few moments … before exhaling. Then open your eyes to break the state.

Part 3

Now for your third positive memory.

Take another slow, deep breath and at the same time close your eyes for a moment. As you exhale, reach back into your mind again and find a positive memory that involves you feeling really good while being spontaneous and in what's often called the 'flow state' or, as sports psychologists call it, the 'zone'.

Perhaps you're involved in a sports activity – like skiing, swimming or running – or maybe you're simply walking or even driving. Whatever the actual activity, there's a part of you calculating everything so fast in 'real time' that you're free to enjoy being completely in the 'Now'. It's almost as though there's another part of you doing most of the work – automatically, intuitively and effortlessly – with you in the flow state and completely present in the moment.

When you've found the memory, I want you to go back into it as though you're really there again, right now; feeling really good, feeling what you felt and enjoying the way you're being. Again, TURN UP the colour and the brightness – making the memory super-real. Feel as though you're really there again, in the 'Now'.

Then take a deep breath right up to the fullest stretch of your lungs; hold it for few moments ... before exhaling. Then open your eyes to break the state.

Part 4

Finally, I'd like you to close your eyes and imagine the person that you really want to be standing in front of you. In your mind's eye, see them clearly right in front of you. Sense and feel all their positive qualities that you aspire to have for yourself.

Now take a step forward into this more positive version of you and 'feel the difference'. Notice a positive shift take place within and straighten your spine. Feel your inner confidence increase as you take a long, slow, deep breath. Hold it a few moments and then let it go; notice how good that feels whilst exhaling. Then open your eyes to break the state.

In future, any time you feel less than your best I want you to take up to three conscious deep breaths – ideally holding each one for up to eight seconds, lifting and straightening your spine at the same time; notice how much better these conscious 'new you' breaths make you feel. More spontaneous, more positive, more confident, more in the present moment, more focused and more empowered. You may not even really know why but you'll just seem to feel so much better after taking them.

You won't need to recall any of those old memories again. You've already done the work involved by searching your memory store and finding the positive resources needed to prepare your lungs for triggering a 'blend' of good feelings that from now on just seem to be there ready to launch at your lungs' fullest stretch.

Practise taking these three deep breaths regularly and by simple repetition, the process will become more and more powerful – it'll serve you well!

Use this exercise as your positive inner switch for snapping out of non-present, anxious or unfocused thinking, and always remember to straighten your spine at the same time as you hold the breaths – it'll give the technique an even more powerful effect. Remember that a count of eight is the ideal length for holding each breath.

Enjoy!

BREATHING PLUS AND THE SUPERNOW

The breath is a fantastic tool – we can do so much more with it than just breathing in the usual way. We can use it for releasing emotions by simply breathing into them, and then exhaling them with our out-breath. We can also use it as I've described here, as a positive state-changing trigger, whenever we want.

It's no wonder smoking tobacco can be such a pleasurable vice. The focus it draws to the breath as a giddy rush of nicotine is sent to the brain had me hooked on smoking two packs a day for a long time. But the long-term benefits of using Breathing Plus make it a far better habit than the potentially fatal long-term effects of breathing poisonous, carcinogenic smoke.

It's a fact: when we breathe slowly, deeply and consciously we are much better able to deal with any situation. It's definitely not our natural response under stress, when we tend to breathe in a very shallow, oxygen-deprived way. Breathing is an essential component to living and health so it really is worth paying more attention to, becoming more mindful of and better at.

I've got two techniques I'd like to introduce, one for you to practise alone in private moments and the second that can be practised covertly in any public situation, and this one is particularly useful for potentially stressful business and social situations.

Both techniques are based on using the breath as the trigger point and, since oxygen helps sharpen the mind and wake you up, both are great for enabling you to be more focused in the moment – awake and alert in the here and now.

THE 'THREE-BREATH' TECHNIQUE

I often call this exercise the 'big guns' of breathing. It's really only effective if you've already done the previous 'stacking anchors' exercise.

During the process I want you to think of your lungs as if they were balloons, with a huge capacity for drawing in that life-giving nectar called oxygen that we're surrounded by (and it's going to seem even more powerful if you do this outside in the fresh air). I recommend you do this alone as otherwise you may attract a few funny looks.

> To start off, take a breath deep into your chest. As your lungs expand like a balloon in all directions, feel them fill out your chest. Take that breath to its maximum point. Fill up your lungs right to the very top. Feel them stretch. Imagine your lungs are like a cathedral that you're filling from the bottom, up to the rafters – with the trigger point up there in the rafters at their very top.

And then hold it ...

Hold it there for at least five to eight seconds but never for more than ten.

You can help improve the trigger point by straightening and lifting your spine.

When you exhale, allow yourself to recover for a few moments before repeating the process twice more.

Notice how your mental state, focus, confidence and clarity improve.

Whenever you do this exercise, stretch up a bit. Make sure your spine is straight and slightly elongated to allow for an unimpeded flow of energy.

Take the air in through your mouth in order to maximize your oxygen uptake. Drink in a breath thirstily to get the oxygen into your lungs as quickly as possible.

The third breath is like the icing on the cake that sets you up for the final payoff. By this breath you should be feeling better than new, and with that oxygen-increased blood making its way around your body you'll feel more consciously awake. Take a moment to notice how good that feels.

On each of the three breaths remain totally focused on the good feelings you've stacked up into the rafters which are now anchored to your lungs, so that each time you hit that high point you're pulling the trigger of your 'big gun' and firing off a round of life-affirming positivity – creating a mighty ripple of wellbeing.

Everybody breathes, but we tend not to give it much thought and the common tendency is to breathe in a shallow kind of way.

Shallow breathing leads to all sorts of health problems. A lack of oxygen can give you the feeling of not really being in your body, a sense of anxiety and feelings of general want and need, when all you actually need is more oxygen.

I remember meeting Ray Mears – the famous TV bushcraft and survival expert. He pointed out to me that you can go for weeks without food if you've got water, days without water, but only a few minutes without oxygen.

When the body feels it's not getting enough oxygen it says it needs something. Sometimes, maybe it's simply a conscious breath or three we really need – rather than the cigarette or the spontaneous shopping spree, food fest or any of the other things we might have a tendency to indulge in when we start feeling we're somehow lacking something deep down.

THE COVERT APPROACH TO CONSCIOUS BREATHING

This is a great way to stay in touch with your breathing when you're in company, and also a great way of improving the power of your communication with others. Try it in a business meeting or any social situation where you're engaged in conversation. This technique revolves around you breathing consciously while involved in listening and speaking.

In order to listen attentively you need to remain awake and alert. In order to be awake and alert you need to be taking in enough oxygen. All our cognitive functions are improved by better oxygen intake. When you go from a stuffy, poorly ventilated room to the outside you'll immediately feel perkier and awake. And if you've had a few too many drinks, a good dose of fresh air will help pull you back into a more sober state. Oxygen is life.

Without losing the thread of the conversation, be aware – or 'mindful' – of how you're breathing when you're talking and listening. When you're talking you have to take a moment between words in order to breathe. The amazing thing is, if you take slightly more significant breaths between sentences you'll feel more inspired and awake, and the way you choose your words will be greatly enhanced.

Rather than snatching breaths as you speak, try occasionally taking a deeper breath and using it to carry your words. Using the breath like this is a very effective way of inspiring the 'flow state' into your conversation.

When you breathe in and consciously hold the breath for a moment while listening to other people speaking, you'll find yourself being more focused and aware of what's really being said.

When I take a deep breath and lift up the top of my lungs, something extra seems to happen. The longer I hold my breath, the greater the release from stress, negative emotion, anxiety and fear that I might be carrying – freeing me to become much more present. Anchoring the positive triggers to the lungs, taking a deep breath and holding and releasing it in the way I've described is what I call Breathing Plus. And the longer you hold the breath, the better you feel when you release it.

When you're feeling particularly wound-up, anxious, fearful or otherwise contrary to how you'd like to be feeling, breathing 'into' these emotions and using the breath to initiate an emotional release can be a revelation in terms of your ability to control how you feel and to have access to a readily available tool that will help you take back that control.

Our cells need just two things to function properly: energy (supplied through the food we eat) and oxygen. Cells need that oxygen in order to release energy from the food. The human body consists of over 75 trillion cells. With every breath you take, oxygen passes through the lungs into the bloodstream; absorbed into the red blood cells, it's then pumped round the body by the heart, supplying and bathing every single cell in your body with the oxygen they need. The cells then give off carbon dioxide which is pumped back around the body on a return trip to the lungs. It's a circle of life that goes on without our having to give it any thought.

Breathing can be done both consciously and unconsciously. Miraculously, there's a part of us that remembers to breathe when we forget.

I've discovered our lungs aren't just there for breathing. The fact is, we have dual-functioning lungs. It's as if they've been designed for two purposes. On a subtle level, they can operate both as a conduit to channel emotions and like a valve for emotional release. As we promote the flow of oxygen through our spinal cord and brains, invigorating the central nervous system as a dynamic channel for change, we're initiating a kind of shape-shifting of our inner being. I believe breath is the key.

Too much negative emotion – anxiety, stress, fear – and too much internal dis-ease can lead to actual disease. The breath offers itself as a way to return to feeling comfortable with 'being', to enable release, help us let go and return to the 'now'. I find myself constantly drifting away from the moment, but by using Breathing Plus I'm brought right back to the present – in a reawakened state.

BEHIND THE BREATH

I like the word 'respiration'; I think it better describes what our lungs actually do than the word 'breathing'. *Spiritus* (Latin for breathing) marks the ebb and flow between conscious breathing and unconscious breathing. Behind the conscious control of your breathing there's a part of you that remembers to breathe when you forget. Among other things, the unconscious part that does this manages and regulates the Autonomic Nervous System (ANS). It's that part of us that looks out for us when we're not looking out for ourselves.

Our breathing is managed by the ANS, which takes care of our body's involuntary activity. The ANS involves both the parasympathetic and the sympathetic nervous systems.

Though it may be called the sympathetic nervous system, this system's not particularly sympathetic to its hosts (you and me) at all. It's the part of our nervous system that deals with the 'fight or flight' response, and the activator of chemicals that cause us to feel anxiety and stress.

The sympathetic nervous system's response, to either real or imagined threats, is to increase the heart rate and blood pressure, restrict breathing, slow down or switch off digestion and stimulate the release of adrenalin and cortisol. These responses are as susceptible to being triggered by thoughts as by real-life events.

When it switches from standby to operational mode, the sympathetic nervous system puts us into a state of immediate high-alert. Even though it catapults us into the present, we're not in the frame of mind that allows us to appreciate being in the moment.

The parasympathetic nervous system, on the other hand, is the part of our nervous system that deals with 'rest and digest' responses, facilitating a deep and satisfying experience of wellbeing. The parasympathetic nervous system comes into play when the body relaxes and when there's no sense of threat. It supports balanced circulation, smooth digestion, and calm and regular breathing. The parasympathetic nervous system is the part of the ANS that underpins our sense of feeling at ease and balanced.

Hypnosis – or the hypnotic trance-state – can help us get closer to the unconscious regulator behind these systems. When you relax, let go and observe your body working all by itself, you'll find that the more you let go, the better you'll feel and doing this regularly will improve your body's immune system.

The unconscious part of the mind is also your source of intuition. It provides you with the support you need to create the conditions for the optimal you. It's right there supplying you with inner help each day and every moment that you step out of the rush of time and settle into the gift of the present.

And remember – wherever there's a gift there's always a giver.

7

FINDING YOUR INNER VALUE

THE VALUE OF SELF-ESTEEM – PRICELESS!

Throughout my life – although it might not have seemed like it from the outside – I've been plagued with feelings of low self-worth. Feelings that were always underscored by a deep sense of insecurity about who I was and how the people I came into contact with perceived me. Looking back, I can trace the source of my uncomfortable self-conscious feelings to when I was about seven or eight years old.

Around this age I remember noticing clear differences among my peers. I began noticing children who had things and children who didn't – children who had more toys and went on better holidays, and those who seemed to have less.

At a relatively early age I became acutely aware that, far from playing on a level playing field, some of my peers were definitely 'more equal' than others. I began noticing what other people had, and it bothered me. I didn't like it when I thought they had more than I did. It seemed to diminish me. It made me feel less than them.

101

Maybe I was picking up on messages being communicated to me through the television and advertising. Maybe it had to do with the affluence of the environment I was being brought up in. Wherever I was getting this from, I became very sensitive to it, and it certainly didn't lighten up as I got older.

I ended up spending a lot of time trying to counter that deep river of insecurity – trying to prove to myself and others that I had value and that I was enough, that I was on at least an even keel with my peers. The thing is, I was always trying to fix inside problems with outside solutions. That said, I guess the solutions seemed to work for a time.

In my attempts to be the best at everything I loved, I became United Kingdom Frisbee Junior Champion in 1975, and then one of the first sponsored skateboarders in Benjyboards, London's premier skate team. I had the need to prove something and went all out to do it, and did it. From sports in my teens to building my business in my twenties, I strove to be the best because the alternative was to have to feel average – which I always equated with feeling 'less than'. Because of my own feelings of insecurity I couldn't just be good at something. I had to drive myself obsessively to be better than everyone else in order to prove to myself that I wasn't worthless and to overcome my feelings of inadequacy, low self-esteem and lack of confidence.

It took me a long time to realize that the external evidence – the better car, the bigger house, the nicer clothes – weren't really solving the deep inner problems. These things were fine in themselves and pretty effective on certain levels, but they didn't cut the mustard in terms of being able to create the conditions for a lasting sense of deep value and self-esteem. Something within was always washing away my attempts at creating a sense of prestige and security.

During the first few years of my recovery, as I did the work I needed to do to get and stay well, I learnt to practise the trance-state and also began to train as a hypnotherapist. I gradually became more and more comfortable with my inner world. Through self-hypnosis I learned to look beneath the surface, listen to my subconscious and tune in to the realm beneath conscious thought.

It was during that time that I realized that my deep core issues could only be solved internally. The fact that I'd been trying to sort them out externally was always going to be the wrong way. Often the last place we go to find the answers we're looking for is inside ourselves, even though they're usually right there for the finding.

Maybe it's easier and more immediate to go out into the world and conquer something, buy something or win something to endorse our sense of self and give our ego a sense of validation. I couldn't stand the sense of feeling 'less than' or 'average'. I didn't even like feeling 'the same as'. I always wanted to feel 'better than'.

In this externally focused culture we're conditioned to look out, to compare and contrast, to assess, judge and, to our own detriment, to play the compare-and-despair game. It took me years to realize the answer was literally right there, under my nose.

I'd heard it before but it had never registered. Gurus, mystics and spiritual teachers often talk about the importance of looking inside ourselves to find the answers. And it was only when I started to do this that I was able to begin to resolve the deep-seated insecurities I had about my own personal value, distortions I'd carried around since I was a child.

There's a commonality that links us all and that connects us with the whole of Nature. It's impossible to find if our attention is focused externally. Maybe it's what's been described as the soul.

It certainly connects us with the infinite and carries with it a profound sense of universal oneness. I know this all sounds rather 'cosmic', but if you look a little deeper you'll find that's exactly what's going on. It's an inside job.

> '*We are like islands in the sea, separate on the surface but connected in the deep.*'
> WILLIAM JAMES

It can happen in a moment of contemplation, when the washing machine of the mind suddenly stops mid-cycle. It can happen in a moment, when we consciously take a deep breath, let go, relax and allow ourselves simply to be present.

It was in a moment like this that I realized to my amazement that I was already perfect, and had been all along. It was a feeling that bubbled up out of the connection I made with the divine realm I found when I went inside. It wasn't the conceited and arrogant voice of my ego.

It was a revelation and, at that moment, the lights came on. All those years I'd been listening to the voice of my insecure ego always comparing me to others and goading me to prove myself better than them. I hadn't realized that self-esteem is impossible to find in the places I was looking, or in the way I was looking.

In that moment I realized there was nothing essentially wrong with me. I was, and always had been, a unique being. In fact, I believe that at the deepest level there's probably nothing wrong with any of us. We're all different, and at the very least perfectly imperfect. Letting go of the struggle in that moment, taking a deep breath and going within, I realized there was nothing I needed to add to myself to feel complete. Just like that, my river of insecurity dried up and suddenly there was no need for anything beyond what I had going on in that moment.

Of course, almost just as suddenly the washing machine came back on, the connection went down and that familiar feeling slowly came back – but not in quite the same way. I'd found something that had shown me a different way. I knew I'd held the secret of self-esteem and I knew that I could find it again because I now knew where to look.

I was on a journey. I realized I'd always been on this journey, but I had never seen it that way. That epiphany made me realize that the important thing was wherever I happened to be on the journey was what my life was all about – not what I had, what I could do, where I'd been or who I'd been with, but where I was in each and every moment of the present. It was not about where I was getting to – the journey itself was my destination.

'Happiness is a journey not a destination.'
CRYSTAL BOYD

We're each of us on our own unique journey. However diverse or different, we're all out here on the high seas making our way in whatever direction we might be heading. And if we don't want to drift aimlessly, passive to the winds and tides, we've got to be able to find our anchor and compass.

In that moment of realization I felt a deep sense of connection to all things and all people. I also realized that the journey was something I had to undertake with total self-commitment. And because of this, taking charge of my vessel depended on me accepting myself as I was, unconditionally. I had to recognize my true value.

I knew I needed to be able to anchor myself to my Self and to find my direction from my inner compass. And while it was singularly my journey, I knew there was also this deep connection with all things, so I didn't need to feel alone in the presence of the great hidden oneness.

A long time ago, a wise old man – now long gone – once said to me, 'Remember, God doesn't make rubbish.' His statement reverberated at a deep level and has continued to make more and more sense.

There's a level on which every life is priceless – feeling and knowing this takes away the need to search for self-esteem. The ultimate secret of self-esteem is that it's not important because you're already priceless. Recognize this, accept yourself as you are and you'll be living your inner value.

That's priceless!

THE IMPORTANCE OF LIVING YOUR VALUES

'Living with integrity means ... behaving in ways that are in harmony with your personal values. Making choices based on what you believe and not what others believe.'

BARBARA DE ANGELIS

To live your values you've got to know what your true value is, and also what your core values are. Acknowledging my core values – and being connected with my inner guidance system as a result

– points me in the right direction and towards the right people and places. In my previous life I may have known what my values were but I wasn't living them. As a result, the people I tended to encounter were not always in my best interest.

From an early age we get exposed to the general values that are core to the society we live in. We also share universal and essential values across our species. Things like being thoughtful to others, of doing to others what you'd like them to do to you, of family, of love and friendship, of believing that giving has its own rewards.

Of course we're all different, and attach value to different principles of living and being, but shared values also unite us across humanity. Whatever your core values are, there's bound to be someone, somewhere else on the globe who shares one or more similar values to your own, even though they may be living a totally different life.

My internal compass helps me steer between what's right and not right for me, generally and in any moment. In the past, I was so focused on the externals that I spent years not even aware that I *had* an inner compass. Not paying attention to your compass can take you anywhere. It got me shipwrecked and very nearly sunk.

Listening to my positive inner voice has given me comfort and guidance, and helped me move forward from one moment to the next. Identifying, acknowledging and living my values helped me become more authentic and true to myself. It has helped me avoid people-pleasing, especially in situations where I've felt I'm being asked to get involved in something that's at odds with what I hold as a core value. Striving to remain true to myself and to my values in this way has sometimes meant I've been misunderstood and even disliked.

LISTING YOUR VALUES

The first step to living your values is to make a list.

Start to think of the qualities you admire in other people. Your list may include things such as integrity, honesty, open-mindedness, considerateness, honour, courage and trustworthiness.

Make a list of all the qualities that you'd want to reflect in your thoughts, words and deeds for you to feel that you are being your very best.

Living the values you choose for yourself will define you.

If you'd like to be loved, one of your values should be to be loving. You need to start by being more loving. And remember, you can't truly love anyone else until you love yourself.

If you want to be respected, one of your values should be to be respectful.

If you want people to be considerate and kind towards you, make consideration of self and others one of the values you choose to live by.

If you want a friend, be a friend.

Make a list of the qualities you admire in other people and the values that you feel are core to you as an individual.

PRACTISING THE ATTITUDE OF GRATITUDE

Rather than comparing and despairing, it makes so much more sense to adopt an attitude of thanks and gratitude for what we actually have rather than fretting over what we don't. The bottom line is, the fact that we're alive and still breathing from one moment to the next is deserving of its own vote of thanks and appreciation.

> *'Any day above ground is a good day.'*
> JAMES REYNE

It's very easy to take the simple things for granted, yet every moment is a miracle in its own right. In the materially focused Western hemisphere we appear to have everything and yet somehow still be blighted. Sometimes the people that appear to have the least seem to be able to be the happiest.

> *'It is only with the heart that one can see rightly. What is essential is invisible to the eye.'*
> ANTOINE DE SAINT EXUPÉRY

We're often so busy looking outward that we can miss the point.

If I don't practise the attitude of gratitude, and instead get back into the habit of thinking about what I *haven't* got and what people *aren't* doing for me, I start to feel bad. Rather than feeling this way, I prefer to think and practise the opposite. It's not about what I'm getting it's about what I'm putting into my relationships, my work and the world around me.

BECOMING OTHER-CENTRED

Becoming more 'other-centred', as opposed to being self-centred, is one of my personal core values and goals.

I find that when I'm outwardly focused – being the best that I can be in that moment – and paying more attention to giving rather than taking, I feel good. And the ego's constant whining 'What about me, me, me?' becomes less and less important.

The ego is wholly self-centred. Other people exist only to fulfil its need for external validation. Surrendering our ego and its obsession with itself, sacrificing this for what we can give to other people and losing ourselves in the process of giving, bring an extraordinary sense of spiritual release. By initiating a loving feeling in myself, I feel a reciprocal sense of being loved.

Whether or not others love you shouldn't matter, but it's really important that you love yourself, with all your human imperfections and flaws. Our society suffers from the disease of perfectionism. In a rather imperfect world, this is a problem.

Surrounded by seemingly perfect manufactured objects – stores stocked with symmetrical produce, fruit and vegetables rejected and dumped if they don't meet exacting standards of visual uniformity, broadcast and print media populated with symmetrically honed, toned and retouched models – feels like it's at odds with Nature.

We live in a world in which things go wrong – we get old and our bodies decay, we have accidents, lightning strikes and volcanoes erupt – life happens. Striving for perfection can only lead to failure and dissatisfaction. Accepting myself unconditionally, as perfectly imperfect, has freed me to be uniquely me – the best that I can be, with no need to have to try to compete and no need to try to be like anyone else. Now I only compete with myself, I'm already a lot better than I used to be.

'Be yourself; everyone else is already taken.'
OSCAR WILDE

If you can accept the imperfections in yourself, you can begin to accept the imperfections in other people. But if you can't forgive yourself, it's unlikely you'll be able to forgive others.

Self-acceptance and self-love pave the way for a healthier, 'other-centred' approach to our relationships, an approach which is devoid of ego-centred judgement, and which accepts people's differences and wherever they might be on their own individual journey.

When adopting this approach I find that the people I interact with respond in unexpected and wonderfully positive ways. It creates its own kind of magic. Operating like this seems to send out a tangible and affirmative ripple. Try it for yourself and see.

In taking the time to read this book (or at least this chapter), if you're not already well under way I'm hoping you might be choosing to begin a new life's work with you as the central focus of the endeavour. Unlike 'project-ego', in which you're the central character of your ego's 'all about me' show, the life's work I am alluding to is art in its purest form – the art of unfolding the divine inner you.

It starts with learning to recognize what you've got, not what your ego thinks is missing – which tends to be the constant subplot of its storyline. Practising the attitude of gratitude is a great way of learning to count your blessings.

Learning to be grateful for what you have, to enjoy being where you are with what you have now, underpins the shift from negative to positive self-perception. Our consumerist society is very effective in making us expert at recognizing and listing everything we haven't got and want, and in encouraging us to feel an uncomfortable sense of emptiness.

With regular practice, getting into the habit of giving thanks, counting your blessings and acknowledging what you've got will slowly transform the way you feel about yourself and your life. It'll definitely make you feel more fulfilled.

There's actual medical research that shows that people who live with a spirit of gratitude have better health, live longer lives and generally seem to enjoy life a whole lot more than those who don't. So it has to be worth trying and even if you almost have to fake it to make it, doing this regularly will soon surprise you.

The attitude of gratitude quite literally dissolves the dissatisfaction that underpins Moreism. When we look at what we've got we'll always feel a whole lot better than when we look at what we haven't got. You have the energy and the life-force, the metabolism and a relative level of health. Whatever level it's at, if you're still breathing and you have life in you you're still in the game.

The attitude of gratitude is such an important discipline I'm going to come back to it in Part Four.

WHAT TO ACCEPT AND WHAT NOT TO ACCEPT

It's crucial to accept the fact that the only person you can really change is yourself, and that essentially you're powerless to change anyone else. However, if you focus on being the best that you can be it's still possible to influence others and play a positive role in their development, but this shouldn't be important. What is important is that in relation to your own process of change and transformation you focus on keeping your own side of the street clean.

Boundaries are fundamental to our maintaining and protecting a deep sense of personal value. And being true to yourself and living your values also sometimes involves standing your ground in relation to the principles that you've identified as being essential.

For our own personal sense of self-worth it's vital we don't encourage or allow others to disrespect us, take us for granted or otherwise walk all over us. Whether they try to or don't is their business. What we're prepared to put up with is ours.

If it's not something you're used to doing, you need to practise learning to stand up for yourself as part of your self-development. We need to be able to say 'no' when we need to in a clear and confident way, so the person we're saying it to is unable to refute our stance. We need to avoid allowing ourselves to be dumped on or downtrodden in any way.

It's more important to be respected than liked. Living your values involves refusing to accept less than your true worth and because you're priceless this means never accepting less than the very best.

In a society dominated by the ego we have to contend with people who will cajole, bully, intimidate and attempt to dominate in order to get whatever they want for themselves. It's important you don't allow these kinds of characters to tread on you. Remember, you're 'equal to all and second to none'.

Some things are not worth losing your serenity over – the queue-jumper, the selfish driver – but if you feel there are core principles at stake, sometimes battles have to be fought. It's a judgement call in relation to the potential consequences to your sanity and serenity, and to your sense of value and self-worth. Sometimes conflict is unavoidable, and when it is it should be faced courageously and intuitively.

Standing your ground is part of your being true to yourself and of honouring your commitment to your personal values.

FINDING YOUR PLACE AND YOUR PURPOSE

I spent years thinking I had to get somewhere else before I could really start enjoying my life. Then I started living my life from a different perspective. I started accepting where I was. I even started being grateful. I acknowledged that, even though it wasn't where I wanted to be on a permanent basis, I was exactly where I needed to be on my journey.

Where you are now is what really matters. Being present in the moment and feeling good about being in the moment is crucial for positive growth. Whatever your circumstances, living with the attitude of gratitude is a very effective way of feeling good about the present moment (crazy as that might seem in some circumstances).

It takes time to achieve a consistent sense of place and purpose and, despite our best intentions, we're going to get blown off course and buffeted by the storms we'll inevitably sail into. Constantly referring to our inner compass and being the best we can be, for both ourselves and those around us, will help keep us facing in the right direction.

Do you have an idea of who you would like to be or of how you'd like to be?

In your mind's eye, can you conjure up a picture of your ideal self?

Can you imagine your ideal self living your core values?

Can you imagine your ideal self acknowledging your feelings and navigating these in order to be the best you can be in each and every moment, even if it means sometimes being misunderstood and disliked?

The following exercise will help you to do this.

I'd recommend that you download the specially created self-hypnosis version of the exercise at www.maxkirsten.com/selfhelpbook, though you can also follow the instructions below.

Take a few moments to clear your mind.

Take a deep breath. Hold it for a moment and then exhale.

Now continue to breathe slowly and consciously.

To begin with, I want you to think of the qualities you most admire in other people, and which hopefully you will have listed after reading the section on living your values earlier in this chapter.

Your list might have included qualities such as honesty, open-mindedness, considerateness, honour, integrity, courage, creativity, trustworthiness – whatever the qualities are that you recognize and value in other people.

I want you to be able to distil these qualities and values, allowing them to be slowly absorbed into your deepest self, so that from now on you'll reflect them in your daily thoughts, words and deeds. Doing this will enable you to feel you are being your very best, optimal, true, ideal and authentic self – and able to keep doing 'the next right thing'. Doing any less would be short-changing yourself.

Take the first quality on your list and think of someone you feel reflects that quality to the core of their being. It may be someone you know personally or it might be someone you've never met but whom you can picture as a living embodiment of the quality.

Imagine that person in front of you. It may be someone you know, someone from history, TV, or the movies. The important thing is that they represent this quality.

Begin to align yourself with them and, in your mind's eye, imagine that the particular quality is magically and invisibly flowing out from them and into you.

Perhaps you can imagine that you can actually perceive the quality with your senses. It may have a colour, a smell or a sound, as well as an actual feeling that you're aware of as it passes out of the person you're imagining and into you.

As the quality moves into you, lift up and straighten your spine and breathe in deeply, imagining the quality travelling with your breath into your lungs and around your entire body.

Hold the breath for a moment and then exhale as you feel the transfer of this particular quality complete.

Repeat the process for each of the qualities on your list, each time selecting someone you feel embodies the particular quality that you would like to be a part of you.

Don't rush to 'break state', and make sure you pause for 30 seconds to a minute between each 'transfer' to fully assimilate each quality, recover physically and prepare for the next quality you're about to process.

As you repeat the exercise you'll begin to feel more positive and confident as the qualities you've chosen become anchored within you. And with this will come a greater sense of the optimal you, able to deal with any situation life may bring your way.

Now I'd like you to imagine the ideal and optimal version of yourself you'd like to be by this time next year. Maybe you'd like to be more positive, to be achieving your goals, being successful, being more creative, being less selfish, more helpful, more confident and more motivated.

In your mind's eye, see yourself as the person you'd like to be in a year's time.

Imagine yourself in the future, exactly as you want to be.

Now imagine this ideal version of yourself standing just inches away, right in front of you. Feel the positive energy coming from the new you. When you're ready, imagine yourself stepping forward and into the future ideal you.

As you step into your ideal positive optimal state, take a deep breath and feel the shift take place. Absorb the new optimal you into your being.

As you exhale, relax and notice how you feel.

Whenever you need to refresh that feeling of the optimal you, take a deep breath and lift your spine. Remembering your vision of your optimal self, imagine yourself absorbing that 'new' you with your breath. Feel yourself facing in the right direction, guided by the core values you've identified as integral components of your true authentic self.

You'll be ready for anything.

ALCOHOL, DRUGS AND OTHER ADDICTIONS – THE 'BLUR'

We live in a society in which deep down a great many of us feel lost and incomplete, in which many of us only feel comfortable when we've taken something to alter our 'regular' state of being. I know all about this, having got to where I am now from a background in which alcohol and drugs played a huge part. Starting at an early age, the idea of getting high – as opposed to feeling low – seemed very attractive. In the environment in which I avoided growing up in the 1970s, it seemed like the perfect thing to do.

Back in the 1970s, recreational drugs were certainly not as entrenched in the cultural fabric as they've since become. The drugs economy was minimal, their quality was generally assured and they possessed a mystique that was very attractive to experimenters in altered states. I'm in no position to cast judgement, because even though my own addictions nearly killed me, they were also an integral part of the journey to where I am now.

It's only a view, but I'd argue that essentially it's not the substances themselves that are the problem, it's what people choose to do with them that lead to addiction. If you're in low-level dis-ease or discomfort – which could be either physical, emotional or spiritual pain – seeking narcotic-induced oblivion can be very seductive. However, if you get used to being in a regular state of 'blur' and if that becomes normal to you, it can be difficult to engage with the real world apart from through the rose-tinted, warm haze that the blur brings.

When I was in that state I was missing out on the potential to experience clarity in the moment – a natural clarity which I've found equals any mood-enhancer, psychedelic, energizer or relaxant I have ever taken.

Dependence on and overuse of any narcotic (including alcohol), particularly over time and as we get older, reaps a savage effect on the body's fine-tuning and energetic balance.

The controlled use of opiates offers very effective pain relief, and both MDMA (ecstasy) and LSD have been used by therapists to enable people to 'find' rather than lose themselves. However, in the Western world narcotics generally tend to be used to get high, to get out of it and 'escape'. In contrast, in the traditional practices of a number of other cultures, psychoactive substances are treated respectfully and with reverence, and used as sacraments to facilitate spiritual experiences and personal transformation. These include ayahuasca, a drink made from visionary plant extracts and used by tribes in the Amazonian rainforests of South America.

It's not just alcohol and drugs that we've got direct 24/7 access to, and can use to take ourselves away from ourselves. Shopping, sex, porn, gambling, even the TV, can all provide their own kinds of distraction from the mundane life-routines of the day-to-day.

Sometimes it can be great to have a holiday from yourself, especially if you've got a tendency to spend too much time in your head getting caught up in excessive thinking. It's just there are potential risks and detrimental physical effects attached to getting caught up in escapist cycles that are likely to develop through regular use of drugs and alcohol or compulsive behaviours.

The blur takes you away from being able to be with yourself on a deep level. When I was getting high on a regular basis, I completely lost touch with who I really was. Without the alcohol or drugs, I found myself living with a stranger within, and there was no way I wanted to be at home with him. It started with me wanting to have a good time, but in the long run my drug use just made the inner struggle worse.

As a teenager, I experimented with drugs for all sorts of reasons. Mostly I wanted to have as good a time as I possibly could, but I was also trying to find myself by testing and stretching the limits of perception and experience. Somewhere along the way, I got lost.

I certainly stretched and tested my limits. I'd pretty much tried everything on offer and been all over the world searching for some kind of solution to the inner turmoil reflected in my life. I was quite a long way down a potentially fatal path before I discovered that the answers I needed were actually hidden inside me all along.

In retrospect I have to say that, because of the dangers attached, it's probably best to get to that place without doing vast quantities of drugs and alcohol. It just so happened that was part of my path to self-discovery. If that's what it takes to begin to look inside, then so be it, but it's an incredibly precarious and potentially hugely destructive path to take, both for yourself and for others in your life.

It's a tricky one: maybe there is a value in losing yourself in order to find yourself, but regularly taking drugs to escape will ultimately lead towards addiction and misery. It's a corrosive cycle. I found that the more I tried to escape, the harder it became to be with myself without the drugs.

I'm the first to admit that mind-numbingly dull, day-to-day routines have the potential to induce low-level depression and a real danger of flicking the switch to permanent autopilot. Narcotics and psychoactive drugs show that behind the veil there's a lot more going on than just 'normal' life, but their regular use runs the risk of dependence.

Far be it for me to denigrate the altered state, but I've discovered some of the highest altered states come from disciplines and techniques which are not reliant on pharmaceuticals. Drugs are just clues to the possibilities of the mind.

These disciplines and techniques are about finding yourself, not losing yourself. They're not going to give you a hangover, risk setting off cancers, cardiac arrest or a stroke, burn out brain cells, or risk creating either a physical dependency or a cyclical pattern of compulsive behaviour.

With a propensity for surfing my way through the various doors of perception, I've discovered meditation and self-hypnosis as techniques to get into deep, naturally induced altered states which overlap in pure and beautiful ways with states and feelings I used to experience on cannabis, ecstasy and opiates.

These states offer the ability to see things very differently and are a natural way to perceive the extraordinary in the ordinary, to wake up to a sense of the divine within and – without the side effects of drugs – have a lasting clarity that enables the ongoing experience of that perception.

8

THE SUCCESS TOOLKIT: YOUR LIST OF ESSENTIAL INNER RESOURCES

Since coming out of the blur of my various addictions, and progressing along the path of recovery, I've identified particular strengths I consider essential for staying in control of my thoughts and actions.

They're interrelated and there is a degree of crossover between each one. Being aware of the potential value of these and working to develop your own toolkit will help you stay on the path to success. They'll support you to maintain an optimal state in order to be the best you can be from moment to moment.

PERSPECTIVE

'The pessimist sees the difficulty in every opportunity; the optimist, the opportunity in every difficulty.'

L P Jacks

Having a good perspective involves seeing things as they actually are rather than seeing a distortion of what is. It's all too easy to slip into catastrophe mode and to over-dramatize situations, overlaying apocalyptic scenarios and predicting negative outcomes when the situation really doesn't merit them. Try to avoid 'catastrophizing'.

In the grand scheme of things, setbacks and difficulties are rarely actual catastrophes or waking nightmares. When we face up to challenges seen in perspective we'll be better able to make it through, and our reward will be a sense of exhilaration and achievement.

Life is difficult. There's no avoiding this uncomfortable fact, but nothing lasts forever and everything is relative. The paradox is that the sooner this difficult truth is accepted, the sooner life no longer seems quite so difficult. The great thing is that we can use the challenges life throws our way to grow into the optimal person we want to become. But it's only possible if we maintain a sense of perspective on what life is bringing our way.

Keep it real. Learn to see things as they are, not as you imagine they are.

COURAGE

> *'Courage is rightly esteemed*
> *the first of human qualities.'*
> Winston Churchill

Having courage complements perspective. The bottom line is having the courage to fail, because if you've tried hard, given something your best shot and hit wide of the target there's still immense value in having been proactive and having aimed high.

The only real failure is not finding the courage to try. Life is all about showing up on the day. It's far worse to fail at something because you didn't have the courage to move beyond the starting gate. At least have a go. Being afraid to play, and allowing your anxiety to get the better of you, is the recipe for deep disappointment in the long term.

> *'To run away from fear is*
> *only to increase it.'*
> Krishnamurti

RESILIENCE

> *'Our greatest glory is not in never falling,*
> *but in rising every time we fall.'*
> Confucius

Resilience is the ability to deal with life. It's the belief that, no matter what happens, you will cope and thrive and that if you get knocked over you'll just bounce back even stronger than before.

Perspective and courage support your resilience to keep going despite the doubts that might creep into your mind. Resilience involves putting up with the forces of resistance and getting on with life anyway.

MENTAL TOUGHNESS

'Where there is no struggle,
there is no strength.'

OPRAH WINFREY

In order to deal with what life can throw at you, having a Teflon-like mental toughness which troubles flow over, round and across but not through, is invaluable.

To be made of tough enough stuff so that when you come up against resistance you don't crumble but meet it in an adaptive way is a great resource for dealing with both challenging situations and people. It's important to be able to stick at things and not give up when first attempts don't work. Mental toughness is all about keeping going.

Change is uncomfortable – mental toughness is indispensable.

POSITIVITY

'There are always flowers for those
who want to see them.'

HENRI MATISSE

A positive mental attitude is essential. There's lots of research that verifies the fundamental importance of maintaining a positive attitude. Positive thought generates beneficial reactions in the chemistry of the brain and body. Being negative brings the whole system down.

*'Positivity adds that extra something
to perspective, enabling you to see things
in the most favourable light – including
life's challenge.'*

M Scott Peck

BELIEF

*'If you think you can do a thing or think you
can't do a thing, you're right.'*

Henry Ford

Hope is useful, but belief is even more important in the positivity stakes. A feeling of hope is a good thing, but belief is much more powerful. It's vital we believe things can get better and that we will prevail.

If you believe you can do something, you're probably right.

FLEXIBILITY

*'Stay committed to your decisions but stay
flexible in your approach.'*

Tom Robbins

When things around you are in a state of flux, having fixed ideas and ways of going about things is not going to help. If you can adapt to unexpected twists and turns, you're evolving in order to survive. Because life is ever changing, it's essential to be flexible.

This includes being able to be flexible with people you come into contact with.

Being flexible involves working with what comes your way rather than predicting what you think should happen and then reacting when it's not what you think it should be. Like the grass and the trees it's important to be able to bend with the forces that inevitably impinge on our day-to-day existence.

In order to be able to bend and not break within we need to be flexible.

Take a lesson from Nature – learn to bend with the breeze, just like the trees.

EXPECTING THE UNEXPECTED!

'To expect the unexpected shows a thoroughly modern intellect.'
OSCAR WILDE

This inner resource supports our ability to be flexible. When you're driving you have to be ready to deal with whatever comes your way – manoeuvring to deal with the ever-changing conditions of the road ahead.

Expecting the unexpected can help you deal with things that happen when you least expect them, and prevents you from being caught off-guard. It involves being present, being alert and being in a state of readiness.

ALWAYS expect the unexpected.

BE LIKE WATER

'Empty your mind – be formless, shapeless, like water. Now you put water into a cup it becomes the cup, you put water into a bottle it becomes the bottle, you put it in a teapot it becomes the teapot. Now water can flow or it can crash. Be like water, my friend.'

BRUCE LEE

Bruce Lee was always one of my heroes. I remember sneaking in to see the film *Enter the Dragon* with my parents (I was under 18) and being completely blown away by his extraordinary martial arts skills. I wanted to be Bruce Lee. I had never seen anyone like him.

In relation to martial arts, he encouraged students not to get stuck in any one form.

'Use no way as the way; have no limitation as your limitation.'

BRUCE LEE

Adapt yourself to what seems to work for you, learn from it and move on.

It's invaluable to learn to flow like water – around, under, over and through – to be able to fit to whatever and wherever we find ourselves.

RELENTLESS COMMITMENT

'The ultimate measure of a man is not where he stands in moments of comfort and convenience, but where he stands at times of challenge and controversy.'

MARTIN LUTHER KING, JR

Whatever the setbacks, you're not going to give up. You're going to confront what's going on and then become even stronger, one way or another.

MOTIVATION

'Success is a state of mind. If you want success, start thinking of yourself as a success.'

DR JOYCE BROTHERS

No procrastinating – you must keep moving. You don't have to rush, just focus on what you need to do today; one day at a time.

PRAGMATISM

'One important key to success is self-confidence. An important key to self-confidence is preparation.'

ARTHUR ASHE

You can suffer short-term discomfort for long-term gain. Whatever it takes, by any means necessary.

RESPONSIBILITY

'When you blame others,
you give up your power to change.'
AUTHOR UNKNOWN

Take responsibility for your thoughts, emotions and actions. Forget the blame culture. You're not a victim, so take back control of your life.

PERSISTENCE

'Many of life's failures are people who
did not realize how close they were to
success when they gave up.'
THOMAS EDISON

You're in this for the long haul. Go at it again and again until you are successful. The only failure is not to try.

The fact that you're still reading this book tells me you're not a quitter.

DETERMINATION

'Strength is a matter of the made-up mind.'
JOHN BEECHER

Maintain an attitude of 'stick-at-it-ness' so that, no matter what, nobody and nothing will put you off achieving your goals.

PART 4

THE POWER OF BEING POSITIVE

'You have to accept whatever comes and the only important thing is that you meet it with the best you have to give.'

ELEANOR ROOSEVELT

How useful would it be if, any time you wished, you could in an instant change your internal state from feeling less than fantastic – negative, nervous, anxious, uncertain or insecure – to feeling your optimum empowered, confident, resourceful, resilient and flowing self? In this part of the book I'm going to introduce you to some simple techniques that will support you in doing just that.

Feeling less than optimal often tends to happen when we get stuck in the past or caught up worrying about the future, or sometimes because we're just not feeling that great. The techniques you'll find in the following pages will help you to snap out of negative feelings. They'll help you find a more positive and resourceful state and also bring you back to being more present in the moment. I spent a lot of time living *for* the moment before turning my life around. Living *in* the moment is very different and, quite literally, inspiring and liberating.

'It takes no time to find yourself.'

ECKHART TOLLE

Being truly present in the moment is where you'll find your Self. Living truly in the present moment will lead you to feeling unencumbered by the past and enjoying the journey towards your future with the best you have to give.

9

BREATHING PLUS AS A POSITIVE INNER SWITCH

'You must live in the present, launch yourself on every wave, find your eternity in each moment.'

HENRY DAVID THOREAU

This technique will allow you to snap back fully into the present. If you're worrying about the past, or anxious about the future, you're not being fully in the present. I've heard it said that anxiety always happens somewhere between now and then. Getting back to the 'now' – which is real – is better than focusing on 'then' – which has yet to happen.

As I mentioned in Part Two, every thought has a physical reaction; worry and anxiety create a sense of unease and physical tension. In order to snap out of this 'non-present' way of being you need to start being more mindful and paying attention to how you feel in the moment and become sensitive to what you're thinking.

'Do not dwell in the past, do not dream of the future, concentrate the mind on the present moment.'

Buddha

When you're not feeling as good as you want to feel stop for a moment. Straighten your spine, lift your posture and draw in a long, slow, deep breath. Hold it in for a calm count of eight. As you count you'll feel a wave of energy flow through you. Allow the extra oxygen carried to your brain by your bloodstream to wake you into the present moment.

Then let the breath go. As you exhale you'll feel more alert and awake, and with that comes a sense of wellbeing and release. Now in the present moment, notice where you are and what you're seeing, hearing and feeling.

Be here now.

I call this technique 'snapping into the present'. It's a fantastic method for 'thought-stopping' anxious, future-based thinking.

The switch of attention has the potential to bring you more fully into the present – feeling the most resourceful you can be and able to deal with what's real, rather than feeling overwhelmed by what you're either remembering in the past or imagining in the future.

It's such a simple and powerful technique yet so easy to forget to do whenever we're feeling less than our best. It's particularly useful for anyone who suffers from anxiety, either of the general or free floating types (where the mind has a tendency to drift into imagined negative outcomes).

Lifting and straightening the spine as you hold your breath improves the flow of life energy – or *chi* as it's called in Traditional Chinese Medicine.

If you practise this technique regularly you'll find it becoming a new positive habit – your positive inner switch.

Lift yourself up into the positive and notice the difference.

THE POSITIVE 'WHAT IF?' EXERCISE: DARE TO DREAM BIG!

'Everything is always created twice, first in your mind and then in reality.'

Steven Covey

If you knew that you couldn't fail, what would you do? Imagine your success and think about it often.

You may not be where you'd like to be. You may not even know where it is you want to get to, but if you start to dream you'll begin to get an idea of where you'd like to be one day.

Begin to imagine the greatest possibilities for yourself. What would make your life more exciting and fulfilling?

Let your imagination run wild, though maybe tempered with a balanced sense of realism.

But don't limit yourself by thinking too small.

By daring to dream big regularly and by adding more and more detail to your dreams you'll be taking the shackles off constrained thought and beginning to imagine the possibilities that you could be heading towards. Imagining something is the first step towards being able to do it. And the steps along the way can become the goals you set yourself as you move ever closer to where you'd like to be.

Try this exercise – you can also download it from www.maxkirsten. com/selfhelpbook.

Take a deep breath and, as you feel the air filling your lungs, straighten your spine and imagine the oxygen you've drawn in shooting up to your brain, allowing your mind to awaken.

Feeling that oxygen rush through your mind, imagine something you'd like to do or achieve. It may be something you've thought about before and perhaps dismissed, or it may be something that just suddenly comes to you, as if from nowhere.

However seemingly ridiculous or unachievable, let yourself imagine it and allow the thoughts to form and sparkle in your mind. However unlikely or outrageous you may think it is, for now at least just imagine it.

Imagine it becoming bigger and brighter in your mind.

Now place it out into the future on the timeline of your life and then imagine yourself doing whatever it is you need to do to achieve this dream.

If training is involved, how long might the training take?

Imagine taking positive action, proactively and persistently repeating whatever it takes to achieve your goal. If you don't know what's involved, imagine yourself online finding out what steps you'll need to take. Let your imagination sparkle as you picture yourself moving towards making this goal a possibility. Perhaps it involves getting hold of information and books, phoning people or communicating via email. In your mind's eye, begin to follow your route towards that dream.

As you imagine it you're embedding the blueprint for your dream in your subconscious mind, getting ready to take the journey and make it a reality.

It might be good to imagine a multiple of dreams. There may be dreams that are just out of the question – I'm never going to be able to break the 100-metre world record, for example – so at this point you should make a judgment call about where you want to put your energy, but don't short-change yourself by dreaming small. Dare to dream BIG!

As you picture the dream in your imagination, break it down from the general to the particular and start to fill in the gaps. If your dream is to write a book, start to imagine the kind of book you'd like to write. What are its themes and, if it's fiction, who are its characters? Imagine writing it.

Following your dreams is so much more fulfilling than not allowing yourself to have any. Having a vision for your life will enable you to see the road ahead. It'll bring value and meaning to your life and give you a sense of purpose.

Everything that exists in the world today began with someone spending time imagining it, dreaming about it and then probably thinking about it a lot. Almost all great achievements begin with a dream.

In 2009, my amazing wife Rebecca was nominated for an Oscar. We were flown, all expenses paid, to the ceremony in Los Angeles (and all the unbelievable parties that went with it). Seated with the other nominees at the front of the awards ceremony, I'll never forget one particular recipient. As she received her Oscar she looked out into the glittering audience. Shaking with emotion, she told us how she couldn't believe she was actually holding the Oscar in her hands and how she'd dreamt about this moment all her life.

It struck me that actually it really wasn't so unbelievable. In fact, if she'd been dreaming about it all her life, it was quite inevitable. She'd probably spent a lot of time going over that scene again and again, dreaming in detail of how she was going to get there.

Imagining that goal in her mind as she headed towards it – thinking about it, dreaming about it again and again and doing a little bit every day to make it a reality until her big dream was no longer a dream.

Why be surprised?

GENERATING MOMENTUM WITH THE POWER OF 'NUDGE'

'The most important thing you can do to achieve your goals is to make sure that as soon as you set them, you immediately begin to create momentum.'

ANTHONY ROBBINS

Having spent time thinking and dreaming about what it is you'd like to achieve, start focusing on it more and more as you go about your day-to-day life. Each day, find ways of moving towards it, sometimes it will be with little steps and sometimes with big strides. Think about what you can do today that could bring you a little closer to achieving your dreams and ambitions.

Take the decision that you're always going to be working towards your dream, and repeatedly nudge yourself towards it. Nudge is the essence of generating momentum. Whether that means writing a sentence, doing a bit of research or having a goals-based conversation with someone, keep doing something every day, or as often as you can, to keep moving forwards.

Ideally you should keep moving towards your goal like a pilot flying a plane towards its destination, constantly readjusting its course and resetting its compass as the plane negotiates the cross-winds it meets en route.

No matter how long or what it takes, just keep heading towards achieving your goals – never forgetting that, just as planes don't fly in straight lines, neither will you.

It's amazing what you can achieve over time by doing a little bit every day.

THE LAW OF THE 'IRREDUCIBLE MINIMUM'

'When patterns are broken,
new worlds emerge.'

Tuli Kupferberg

There may, however, be times when you feel stuck, blocked or even paralysed with fear. You may feel that you're unable to develop any momentum or that you can't even seem to get started. Rather than getting frustrated, begin to chip away at the tasks involved. Ask yourself, 'What's the very least I can do?'

Years ago, I was first taught the law of the 'irreducible minimum' by Danny from Florida, a wonderful old man and friend, who's sadly no longer with us. He suggested that if you feel blocked, stuck or unable to build any kind of momentum, ask yourself – 'What's the very least I can do today or, better still, right now? What's the absolute minimum positive action I can take towards achieving my goal?'

There may be a phone call you need to make that you're putting off because you don't feel right and you're worried the conversation won't go the way you'd like it to. Well, you don't have to make it, but you could get things ready for the call, as if you were going to make it. You could jot down a few notes about what it is you want to say so you're fully prepared for the conversation. Think about the main points you want to put across and note them down.

You could get the phone number ready and prepare the conditions to make the call. Decide where you'd like to make it from. Get the chair you'd like to sit on while making the call (though some calls are best made standing up with a confident posture). Switch off all potential distractions that could ruin the call.

If I were going through this process, and even though I'd still not be committed to making the call, I'd probably start preparing my internal state. I might use the positive inner switch to get into the optimum confident internal state and bring myself into the present instead of worrying about the call and imagining it not going well.

Whatever it is that's blocking me from making the call, by taking a few deep breaths and becoming present I'd be getting myself into a more confident state from which I'd feel readier than I'd ever felt to actually make the call. This would be a great opportunity to put Breathing Plus into action.

I might put the phone in my hand, even though I might not actually make the call. I might even dial the number, knowing that I didn't have to get to the point where I could hear the ring tone.

When you've gone so far towards doing a task you feel blocked about, use the positive inner switch to feel good about where you are and what you're almost ready to do.

At this point I might take a deep breath and dial the number. I could allow the phone on the other end of the line to ring, even though I could still hang up if the person answers, though by now I might feel ready to follow through and actually have the conversation.

'Come to the edge, he said. They said: We are afraid. Come to the edge, he said. They came. He pushed them and they flew.'

Apollinaire

Whatever it is you're feeling stuck with, try breaking it down to the absolute irreducible minimum.

You may be feeling overwhelmed by the thought of having to clean your home, but if you just pick one room and begin there, at least you'll feel better about having done something. Having done one room you might feel able to carry on, or you may decide to come back to the task and continue at another time.

Approach tasks that have been broken down into much smaller chunks in order to start building even the smallest degree of momentum, and then use the power of nudge to continue the momentum.

Doing things in manageable chunks will enable you to maintain control of your mental, physiological and spiritual state, rather than feeling overwhelmed and not in control. If, for whatever reason, you're not ready to begin at least you can *prepare* to begin. Procrastination causes frustration and kills momentum, and because avoidance causes dissatisfaction, rather than not doing something, begin with the smallest step you can.

Commit to taking back control and create the minimum amount of momentum towards doing what you need to do.

And if you're putting off doing things you need to do in order to do things you enjoy doing – get those things you need to do out of the way first. Defer gratification. You'll be able to enjoy doing the things you like doing even more, without that nagging sense of guilt at the back of your mind.

I recently used the law of the irreducible minimum to help the pop star, Peter Andre, overcome his fear of heights and roller-coaster rides. He wanted to take 'Saw', one of the latest and most terrifying roller-coaster rides at Thorpe Park, but had had a morbid fear of roller-coasters since having a panic attack on one some years back. He also wanted to film the occasion for his reality TV series. Even after several sessions of hypnotherapy, and some focused mental preparation, Peter was still unable to get on the ride. He wanted to, but felt stuck.

I suggested he just climb the stairs and look at the ride's seating pods, without thinking he had to actually go through with the ride. At the top of the stairs, I suggested we sit in one of the seats at the front to see how it felt, and also for the photographer to get a shot of him, again with the knowledge that he didn't *have* to go any further if he didn't want to. When he was sitting in the front row of the ride, I asked him to imagine how good it would feel if he actually took the ride and walked away triumphant, knowing that he'd overcome his fear.

He suddenly said he'd do it if I would, too – OMG! So together we took one hell of a deep breath and found ourselves plummeting down a 100-foot beyond-vertical drop and speeding through a series of death-defying inversions. Returning to the platform when the ride was over, Peter turned to me and said that he could probably do it again, and maybe this time he'd actually be able to enjoy it.

Peter had a very real phobia, but it was the idea of it in his *mind* that was troubling him, rather than the actual reality of the situation. By approaching the task a little at a time, he was able to take himself through his phobia and come out the other side knowing that he'd taken back control.

MORE ABOUT PRACTISING THE ATTITUDE OF GRATITUDE

'Gratitude unlocks the fullness of life. It turns what we have into enough, and more. It turns denial into acceptance, chaos to order, confusion to clarity. It can turn a meal into a feast, a house into a home, a stranger into a friend. Gratitude makes sense of our past, brings peace for today, and creates a vision for tomorrow.'

MELODY BEATTIE

If you have a natural disposition towards thinking of the half-empty glass – if you have a tendency to feel resentful, negative, generally dissatisfied and downtrodden – regularly practising the attitude of gratitude will help you start feeling much better about your lot in life. It'll start to reprogramme your mind to think in terms of your glass being half-full, and draw your attention towards all that you have in your life rather than what you don't have. Don't play compare/despair, instead be glad for what you've got.

Practising the attitude of gratitude involves looking for the good in everything rather than immediately identifying the negative. Looking for the good in things creates positive energy and good feelings. Switching from a negative point of view to a positive perspective will pull you into the positive and towards an optimal state, and feeling fulfilled rather than incomplete. Remember, it's difficult to feel grateful if you're stressed, so when you feel like you're going under take a deep breath and think about how far you've come.

There are some who might argue that being 'pessimistically optimistic' is a better way of being, hoping for the best but preparing for the worst. I tend to think that having a foot in both camps isn't really being committed enough to the positive.

If you need to reprogramme yourself to think in terms of the half-full glass, start to develop an attitude of gratitude.

To get into the habit, I recommend you do this:

- Each day, make a list. Actually write down on a piece of paper at least 10 to 20 things that you're grateful for. You might start with your health, your body (the parts that still work!), your family, your friends, the fact that you're eating regularly and that you hopefully have a bed to sleep in. Whatever your circumstances, you can choose to have a positive perspective.

In NLP terms, shifting your perspective to the positive is called *reframing*.

If you make a list, before you've even finished you'll be feeling a whole lot better than when you started. Right now you may not have everything you want but you can still be grateful for what you've got. I may not have a 'super car' but the one I've got is reasonable enough – well, it was. Involved in an accident a few weeks ago, my car was completely written off while I was returning from my mother's hospice just before she passed away. I walked away, badly shaken but not hurt. Now that *is* something to be grateful for.

Sometimes I have to really work at it, but practising the attitude of gratitude makes me feel so much better than in the past when I used to feel miserable, discontented, hard done by and worried that I wouldn't get everything I wanted. The fact is, most of the time I pretty much have what I need, and that's something I can be extremely grateful for.

Acknowledging this stops me from feeling that I'm a victim of life. Sure, life happens. Sometimes it's up and sometimes it's down, but practising the attitude of gratitude and focusing on the positive makes me more resilient to whatever comes my way.

Having nearly lost my life in the past on quite a few occasions, now when I wake up in the morning I often say to the universe, 'Thank you for another new day of life.' It's a great place to start the day from. I used to find it really hard to recognize what I'd got in my life rather than what I hadn't got, but these days life feels so much more precious.

'Everything we do should be a result of our gratitude for what God has done for us.'

LAURYN HILL

We get what we get.

The ultimate attitude of gratitude is being able to say with sincerity – 'Thank you for everything that you've given me and everything that you've taken away.'

BEING HAPPY

> *'Most folks are about as happy as they make up their minds to be.'*
>
> ABRAHAM LINCOLN

Regularly practising the attitude of gratitude will bring you greater happiness. Being alive isn't a permanent condition, and life is difficult and ever changing. However, appreciating the simple things can lead to a sense of happiness, and a joy in simply 'being'. Lasting happiness isn't about where you're living or the car you're driving. It begins by getting your head right and by getting yourself right. Make up your mind to be happy and fit yourself to life. Remember, it could always be worse.

Living in the moment doesn't necessarily mean you're always going to be happy. As Buddha pointed out, suffering is very much a part of life. Having things is great, but the good feelings they can bring only go so far, and we can't pin our happiness on them. We've got access to so much stuff in our society, yet find it hard to enjoy simply being. Compared to other places in the world where people have so much less yet seem far more content, we in the West still have a lot to learn.

'The more you know the less you need.'

OLD ABORIGINAL SAYING

Even if you're not where you'd like to be yet, you can still be happy with where you are on your journey and content to 'trudge the road of happy destiny' – as they say in the AA 'Big Book' – on the great adventure with the rest of us on the same spiritual path.

10

BEING AUTHENTIC AND TRUE

'Neither do people light a lamp and put it under a bowl. Instead they put it on its stand, and it gives light to everyone in the house.'

MATTHEW 5.15 (NEW INTERNATIONAL BIBLE)

You've probably heard the saying 'don't hide your light under a bushel'. Being authentic and true is all about being comfortable with who you are, and confidently letting yourself shine. It's really important to be able to live with the feeling that you're right with yourself and the world.

Feeling fulfilled requires the right state of mind and depends on being able to find a position of alignment with a number of crucial elements, including being present, daring to reach for your dreams, being grateful, liking who you are, being positive, being authentic, being true to yourself, feeling that something remarkable is going on from the inside out. But most of all, giving something back to others because when we give, we receive. Remember that giving has its own reward.

'As we let our own light shine, we subconsciously give other people permission to do the same.'

Marianne Williamson

You've probably also heard the old saying 'to thine own Self be true'. Being who you are from the inside out will give your personality a foundation of solid rock. In a world in which so many people are acting or pretending, and building houses on sand that are never going to be storm-worthy, it can sometimes be difficult to let go of the feeling that, as we are, we're somehow not good enough. By being authentic and true to yourself you'll be on unshakeable ground.

And never forget – nobody can be you better than you can.

In the past, before my new life, I always used to feel that I was somehow going to be uncovered as a fraud (not surprising really as I was always up to something or other, or trying to be someone I wasn't). I had this fear that people would suddenly start asking 'Who the hell is this guy and how the hell did he get into the room?' I didn't feel authentic. Disconnected from my inner realm, I was projecting myself from the surface. Once I'd learned how to overcome my self-doubt and let my authentic self shine through, the fear of being found out disappeared.

Thankfully I no longer need to self-medicate in order to feel comfortable. These days I've got rid of all the props and found out who I am by doing the 'work' I needed to do. Following the techniques I've outlined in this book – clearing the wreckage of my past, overcoming the fears and doubts that kept me caught up in all my addictions, living by my values, using my success toolkit to help me be the best I can be each day has been essential. Obviously some days I'm better than others, but so long as I'm still on the path, each day is a success.

Go beyond your ego's chatter and listen to your heart. Being authentic and true will give you a deep sense of balance and strength.

We're all made of stardust so let your light shine.

WELLBEING AND BEING WELL

*'The part can never be well
unless the whole is well.'*

Plato

Being 'well' means having a feeling of being positively right with the world in the moment. It involves being authentic, feeling valued, taking care of your body and being conscious of being connected to something spiritual – whatever that something is for you.

I believe we feel a greater sense of wellbeing when we're looking after those three overlapping areas that create health in our lives: the mental, physical and spiritual. We feel it most when we're practising self-care and achieving a balance between the three areas of our being. Neglect any one of them at your peril. Like a three-legged stool, remove one and balance becomes difficult, if not impossible.

YOUR WELLBEING SURVEY

Take a wellbeing survey. On a scale of 1 to 10, how would you rate your overall sense of wellbeing at this moment? Ask yourself two questions:

How am I? ☐ /10

How am I feeling? ☐ /10

Here's a small exercise:

Find a moment when you're not suddenly going to be interrupted and take a deep breath. Hold the breath for a count of eight and let your body relax as you exhale and let the breath go.

Begin to search your internal condition.

Out of ten how are you feeling on the mental level? Do you feel at all resentful – of people, places or things? Are you poisoning yourself with resentment? If you are it'll be impeding your joy of living and sense of wellbeing. ☐ /10

Out of ten how are you feeling on the spiritual level? How are you with your spirituality? Do you believe you have a spiritual dimension? Is there something or nothing? If you think there is something, what is your alignment with it? And are you being true to yourself and your values with that? If you think there isn't anything, that's OK, too. Atheists can still believe in pragmatism, in doing the right thing and in the fundamental beliefs of humanism. Maybe dogma and religion turn you off the idea of the spiritual; it doesn't matter. The crucial thing is to feel positively aligned with the values that are important to you. ☐ /10

Out of ten how are you on the physical level? Are you looking after yourself physically? Are you eating a regular, balanced and nourishing diet? Are you getting enough sleep? Are you ensuring you get exercise? ☐ /10

Check yourself in relation to this inner audit. Take stock of your credits, debits and balances, and use this book and the hypnosis NLP downloads to create the ideal conditions for your wellbeing. And don't forget, being truly well – mentally, physically and spiritually – depends on your finding your inner connection, and a sense of comfort in being with your inner self.

11

SELF-HYPNOSIS

'Healing by trance-state (or an altered state of awareness) is among the oldest phenomena known to man and is found in one form or another in virtually every culture throughout the world.'

WILLIAM BROOM

Coming through my personal abyss, going through the process of conquering all my addictions, fears and anxieties and finding myself in recovery and becoming well, I discovered hypnosis was a wonderfully effective way of helping me overcome some of the things I was having difficulty shaking off. These included quitting smoking and conquering my feelings of stress and anxiety. Rather than trying to deal with my issues from the outside, as I'd always tried to before, hypnotherapy enabled me to make the necessary changes from within.

In the process I discovered I really loved being in the trance-state so I trained to become a hypnotherapist myself. I found that being in trance didn't in any way make me feel that I had lost control. It was through hypnotherapy that I was able to find my inner Self and make friends with that part of me that had always been a stranger.

Self-hypnosis involves creating a state in which you become relaxed and beyond the worries and cares of the everyday world. I like to call this being in the 'state of beyond caring'. By following the exercises in this book (and regularly listening to my hypnosis NLP downloads) you'll be learning techniques for self-hypnosis. It's a wonderful method for becoming more balanced. Hypnosis certainly helped me to get myself right, and self-hypnosis is something I now practise daily.

I think everyone should learn how to do self-hypnosis or meditation and practise regularly. Though essentially they are quite different, there are great similarities between them and the health benefits overlap. Like hypnosis, meditation is a great way to get beneath the surface, observe what's going on, learn to just 'be' and develop a deeper awareness of things as you become more mindful and present.

THE EXTRAORDINARY EFFECT OF PRAYER AND MEDITATION

'Prayer is when you talk to God; meditation is when you listen to God.'

AUTHOR UNKNOWN

If prayer is talking to God – Nature, the universe, your higher self, whatever you want to call it – meditation is the opposite. It's about being still and listening quietly. Both, however, are forms of communication.

So why practise prayer and meditation, particularly if you're agnostic or even an atheist?

If you've got a 'scientific' mind, you may have difficulty in finding value in the unquantifiable. But even if you are this way inclined, and don't have a belief in a divine presence, there's still great benefit to be had from the act of prayer and the practice of meditation. Begin with an open mind, avoiding contempt prior to investigation.

The fact is, the way I approach prayer and meditation has nothing to do with religious doctrine. I've found it personally more useful to develop my own relationship with an unseen power and in a more mystical sense than might be the case if I'd sought it through a church or religion-based concept of the divine.

The important thing is that your prayer and meditation should be genuine, true and come from the heart.

With prayer, it's important to be able to let go of the expectation of an end result and open up to whatever the outcome might be – so be careful about asking for specifics. Both prayer and meditation can be tremendously empowering. They can provide comfort, a sense of connection, the support to overcome fears and doubts and help to achieve extraordinary things.

For some people the idea may seem a little scary or even ridiculous, but I recommend having an open mind – beware of contempt prior to investigation. Don't analyse, just try. Act as if there really is an infinite power everywhere. Learn how to use 'the force' not unlike the Jedi Knights in *Star Wars*.

At sports and athletics events you'll often see winning athletes (particularly the ones setting new world records) pointing or looking to the sky, making a symbol that implies they have a relationship with something 'greater' than themselves and acknowledging the power that's helped them reach further than they'd normally reach without it.

Meditation can really help if you feel the inner you is a total stranger and if you find it hard to be alone with yourself. Just sitting in stillness and listening can bring a deep sense of oneness and connectedness to the unseen power within – the power greater than you that some people call God and others prefer to call 'good orderly direction' or the higher power.

Whatever you want to call it, it isn't you at the level of your conscious ego but it is still there, just below the surface of your conscious awareness. All you have to do is look a little deeper in a moment of stillness and calm. In time you'll be able to feel it beneath the level of your conscious mind.

Meditation will enable you to observe what's going on within without getting caught up in the mind's tendency to move from thought to thought. It'll help you to view your thoughts like clouds, drifting across the clear sky of your mind with no more substance than that which you give them.

And if you're looking for illumination and enlightenment through meditation, there are many approaches and wonderful ways into the practice which you could explore. It's not a complicated or mysterious thing to do. Read through the exercise below and try it out. It's a simple meditation, and you'll soon start to notice the benefits if you do it every day.

Find somewhere quiet and where you'll be free from distractions.

You can lie down or sit, but make sure your spine is straight.

Close your eyes and breathe slowly and deeply.

Notice your body and your senses.

Be aware of what you can hear, smell and feel around you.

Be still and observe.

Be.

Don't think about what you're sensing and feeling – just observe it.

Notice your breathing. There's no need to do anything with it, just be aware of the sensation as the breath enters and leaves your body.

Keep your attention on your breath and each time your mind wanders elsewhere, gently bring it back.

Feel your breath as it enters and leaves your body.

Enjoy this special time.

I'd recommend you do this for 10 to 20 minutes every day. If you find that a bit of a challenge, practise for as long as you can and build up the length of time you can manage.

FINDING YOUR SELF

'Your work is to discover your world and then with all your heart give yourself to it.'

BUDDHA

I'd like to make a distinction between the Self that this book's title refers to and the ego-based self that's behind the self-centred and self-obsessed chatter in our minds. The ego-based self is often prone to disappointment and to feelings of self-doubt. It either feels better or worse when it compares itself to others, but it mostly feels unfulfilled. The Self I'm referring to is another part of you. It's the Self that helps you to do things and to remember the things that matter. I used to say it's the part of you that gets you home safely when you've got no recollection of how you did that. It's been looking out for you all your life.

Finding your Self isn't about getting self-obsessed and caught in a narcissistic loop. This isn't the 'all about me' show. Nor is it the 'ism' in Moreism – the 'I', 'self', 'me' that leads to discomfort, a feeling of lack or dis-ease and a craving for comfort and distraction and for seeking external solutions as fixes for internal problems (sometimes called 'self-soothing' in the addictions-recovery world). The real answer lies in finding internal solutions for the issues going on inside. And these solutions depend on you finding your inner Self.

It's often that part of themselves that many people can't bear to be with. Lots of people spend a lot of time keeping busy – always out and about and unable to cope with being at home on their own, always trying to escape their feelings. Essentially it's where Moreism, alcoholism, shopping, drugs and addictive behaviours of all kinds start. All of these are ways of escaping your inner Self.

The key is to learn how to become comfortable with the stranger within – with the part of you that you may least want to be alone with. The fact is the solution lies in making friends with that part of you and with becoming familiar and comfortable with your inner Self. This is the part of you that has always been just beneath your conscious awareness, giving you intuition and guidance. It's always been there helping you in the background. That stranger is actually your friend.

Hypnosis works by accessing the subconscious, a realm of the mind that lies just below the conscious mind. Once you start spending time with your inner Self, you'll begin to find you're more and more comfortable with both the conscious and subconscious realms of your mind, and able to have direct access to the ocean of the unconscious.

The subconscious acts as a gateway, or channel between the conscious mind and the unconscious. The unconscious is the vast (possibly infinite) realm of your mind which your dreams, ideas, inherent creativity and intuition bubble up from. Becoming open to this inner realm will begin to give you a sense of wholeness and of being complete, and a connection to the infinite. This is the Self I'm talking about.

By making it your best friend and ally, this part of you will give you the support you need to get through the inevitable trials life brings. Learning to relax, spending time being with yourself, and getting into the habit of self-hypnosis or meditation can help you find and get to know your Self in a wonderful way.

PART 5

LIVING LIFE FROM NOW

THE 'NORMAL' NOW AND THE SUPERNOW

Sometimes life can seem rather dull, flat and boring. The mundane day-to-day chores and the routines of work are all things we probably find little pleasure in doing. In this book's Introduction I mentioned the ongoing nature of the work involved in creating the person you'd like to be, and the importance of doing the work to become your ideal, positive, confident and integrated self. However, without noticing it it's likely you'll keep drifting away from your new illuminated and inspired state – in which you're 'awakened' and fully aware of the wonders of life – into what I call the 'normal' now: that 'regular', 'nothing's amazing', 'so what?' kind of feeling can easily creep back up on us.

In Part Three I introduced the concept of being in control of changing states at will – from feeling as if you're in a state of negative 'lack' to a feeling of positive 'plus'. The anchoring process I explained and outlined as a technique for doing this can be used again and again to build up more and more positive triggers that you can use to quickly change how you feel. Using the triggers regularly and developing the practice of state-changing as a habit will take those neural pathways up to superhighway status and make state-changing easier and easier. State-changing exercises are the keys to transforming the 'normal' now into what I call the SuperNow – the awakened state in which you can find and truly appreciate 'the extraordinary in the ordinary'.

A renowned Zen master was once asked by one of his pupils what Zen is. The master smiled and replied 'chopping wood and carrying water'. The simplicity of his answer hides the key to enlightenment. It's not the activity that matters, but the inner state of the person carrying out the activity. Mundane tasks are only mundane when you're in the 'normal' now. In the SuperNow the realization of the extraordinariness of your own existence raises the level of consciousness towards enlightenment. The Breathing

Plus exercises I introduced in Part Three are great ways of shifting into the SuperNow, raising the level of your consciousness and creating an enlightened state of joy in simply being and doing.

As well as giving our lives a decidedly dull edge, feelings of drudgery and monotony have their own side effects.

> *'Stress is caused by being "here"*
> *but wanting to be "there".'*
>
> ECKHART TOLLE

Though few live there permanently, with practice we can live in the SuperNow more and more. Shifting between the two versions of the 'now' is important. If we were permanently in the SuperNow it could lose its extraordinary value and become normal. After all, what's light without the dark to compare it to?

> *'All sun and no rain makes a desert.'*
>
> ANON

12

LIVING SUCCESS AND THE IMPORTANCE OF SELF-MAINTENANCE

'Success is not the key to happiness; happiness is the key to success. If you love what you are doing, you will be successful.'

HERMAN CAIN

It seems as though we're now living in a blame culture, and if you're currently subscribing to this you need to step away and stop following the blame cattle. Don't allow yourself to be drawn into the blame game. As I said before, it takes your power and turns you into a victim – never forget the old saying 'one finger pointing at others, three fingers pointing back at you'. Give the old blame game the two fingers and take responsibility for achieving your own success.

There's really only one person you can continue to change on your journey and that's yourself. So thumbs up for taking responsibility for yourself. Use the tools for success outlined in Part Three – particularly commitment, determination, resilience, adaptiveness and flexibility.

The people who have obituaries written about them are generally individuals who've made a significant contribution to society. If you want to achieve success, ask yourself how you can be of most use to other people, to society, to your country or to the rest of the world. It's not so much about what people can do for you, it's about what you can do for other people. Success often comes as a result of being able to identify a need that other people have and then finding and developing a new solution, or a better service or product, to fulfil it.

Let other-centredness rather than self-centredness be your motivation for success. Be significant to others.

'Success is a journey, not a destination.'
ARTHUR ASHE

CONTINUING TO TAKE PERSONAL INVENTORIES

On life's great journey it's important to continue to take a regular personal inventory, and when you find you're somehow going wrong to promptly admit it. At times of significant disturbance in your life you may find it helpful to repeat the 'dark lists' exercise – not forgetting to balance these by also doing the light lists. Don't approach doing the lists as a 'one-off'. Taking simple, regular inventory should become part of your life's process. Each time you take an inventory it'll help you see things more clearly and give you the ability to identify what's your 'stuff' and what belongs to other people. As I've mentioned before, it's important to regularly keep your own side of the street as clean as possible and to accept that none of us is perfect.

Sadly, I myself am still far from perfect, and my wife would be only too happy to confirm this as a fact – if I hadn't made her sign a non-disclosure agreement! The important thing is that we're doing our best. However, on some days we're definitely better than on others. It almost seems as though we have to take turns at being at our best on different days, and that perhaps being 'perfectly imperfect' is the best we can hope for – always remembering that it's never too late to start your day again if things all go pear-shaped. Just take a deep breath, get things back into perspective and begin again. It's also important to remember that 'sorry' is not simply a word but an amended way of behaving – directly or indirectly – towards the people we care about.

THE IMPORTANCE OF 'OTHER-CENTREDNESS' IN OUR SELFISH SOCIETY

Being other-centred is central to happiness. Research has shown that putting others first can, among other things, help ward off depression. Being other-centred is the opposite of being self-centred, thinking only about yourself in relation to everyone and everything.

In the modern, capitalist Western world, 'Moreism' acts as the driver of excessive consumption. It's pretty much impossible to escape our almost constant bombardment by myriad forms of advertising telling us that we need things in order to feel more complete. Advertising agencies have learned from psychologists that the key to selling is to create a sense of need in a target market which their product can appear to have the power to satisfy. What's more, by creating dissatisfaction with what we have, we're being programmed to want more.

During the process of my own recovery I discovered that the solution to restless dissatisfaction and almost terminal self-centredness required shifting my selfish focus away from a feeling of unquenchable need to one of other-centredness. The original AA 'Big Book' goes even further, saying that 'our very lives … depend upon our constant thought of others and how we might help their needs.' I would highly recommend that we take these worries and adapt them to our lives.

And don't forget, your success can be enhanced if you ask a power greater than yourself how you can be of use to the human race.

ACKNOWLEDGING THE 'GIFT OF GRACE'

'Amazing grace, how sweet the sound, that saved a wretch like me … I once was lost but now am found, was blind but now I see.'

JOHN NEWTON

When you stop and really think about it, it's amazing how our body's various systems somehow repair, renew and protect us. It's as though we've a part of ourselves that looks after us and even looks out for us. There's so much more to us than what we're usually conscious of. It also seems as though we've got inner senses – including the mysterious sense of intuition – that somehow dramatically, and often just in time, intervene to avert a major disaster, saving us whenever it can.

If you think about how many close shaves we've all had during our lives – all the times we've somehow, just in time, stepped back from the speeding car, survived a terrible accident, nearly fallen from a window or nearly done something fatal – you have to agree it's quite amazing any of us are still alive. I also know that terrible accidents take place and bad things can and do happen to some of us. Yet somehow it is possible, if we survive, to come through these experiences enriched, wiser and 'better'. We can use our experiences in life to help us evolve as individual beings.

I know that in my case I have been more than lucky. The number of incidents I shouldn't have survived is extraordinary. For some reason I've been able to recover from my addictions and afflictions – seemingly more by grace than good judgement – one day at a time. I also know that this freedom from my various addictions, the 'new me' that I've chosen to become and my better, improving life, is truly a gift.

Who, how or what is behind these seemingly divine interventions is less important than just noticing the many incidents of 'grace' that just happen in our lives. I know that most young people feel that they're immortal and going to live forever; that they won't get lung cancer from smoking or that they won't come unstuck when others did – that they're the exception rather than the rule. I can't believe that I took some of the world's most addictive drugs, truly believing that I wouldn't get addicted, and that I was stronger than the drugs that had enslaved so many. What was I thinking? Why was I one of the few lucky enough to survive all my addictions when many I knew didn't make it?

It really is by the gift of grace that I'm here to write this book today. Look for the ways in which grace has touched your own life.

THE IMPORTANCE OF NATURE

'If we could see the miracle of a single flower, our whole life would change.'

Buddha

Growing up in London in the seventies, the school I disliked going to the most was thoroughly modern – made of concrete with no trees or grass. It had sunken concrete playgrounds and a high level of violence. Whether it's as a reaction to that environment or something more innate, even though I was brought up in the city I've always loved parks, rivers and trees.

When I was at my most unwell and lost in my addictions, I became almost totally detached and often felt separated from Nature. I felt strangely uncomfortable when I was in the countryside and could never wait to get back to the city again. Since recovering, though, I've learned the importance of having a relationship with Nature.

When I first gave up smoking cigarettes I bought a bonsai tree (a Japanese miniature tree). Being an addict I soon built up a huge collection. As I watched them going through their seasonal changes and developed a relationship with them, I began to realize that the connection I needed with them was as important as the connection they needed with me, as their carer.

It's no surprise that we take flowers to people when they're sick, and that hospices are often designed to incorporate beautiful gardens. Trinity Hospice, Clapham – where my mother ended her days while I was still writing this book – is beautifully landscaped to reflect Nature's infinite quality and even has a pond with koi carp.

By connecting with Nature we're connecting with the infinite, and if you have an ongoing and special relationship with Nature – whether it's growing bonsai trees, gardening or caring for a pet – you'll be both enriching the quality of your life and extending its length, and there's now scientific proof of this.

FINDING THE INFINITE EVERYWHERE

'To see a World in a Grain of Sand,
And a Heaven in a Wild Flower,
Hold Infinity in the palm of your hand,
And Eternity in an hour'

WILLIAM BLAKE

Having a relationship with nature is one of the keys to wellbeing, balance and happiness. When you learn to look deeper into all living things you'll be able to see the 'circle of life' and find your own part in the great oneness that so many people fail to make the time to experience.

A LESSON FROM THE SAMURAI WARRIORS

'Always keep in mind: We are mortal. Our
life is short. Everything we do has eternal
significance. Those who live well, die well'

PAUL WASHER

Samurai warriors in ancient Japan were taught to keep the thought of death in mind at all times. That meant every day and every night, 24/7. This practice is based on the belief that if you do this, you'll treat each day as more precious and your relationships with friends and loved ones as worthy of greater attention and value. It's also based on the belief that, with death in mind, you're less likely to waste energy on the unnecessary, you will keep things in perspective, won't get involved in futile arguments and will avoid going places where you might end up getting into trouble.

It's a way of thinking that'll help to curb all excessive behaviour, whether that's over-eating, over-indulging in sex or getting caught up in the kinds of addictive behaviours I was involved in. Excessive behaviour is bad for the body and can lead to a premature death or a disabling condition. If you keep death in mind, you're more likely to live a moderate life, look after yourself and live longer.

When people don't keep death in mind and act as though they're going to live forever, it's easy for them to get overly attached to things, have a tendency to Moreism and forget that they can't take anything with them when they die.

Life is short. Accepting the inevitability of death and seeing the value of each day, and living each as though it's your last with love, honour, courage and 'presentness', is the way of the samurai warrior. We're alive today but have no idea whether or not we're going to be here tomorrow.

Keep death in mind – one way or another it'll improve your character. Life is precious.

> *'Live as if you were to die tomorrow.*
> *Learn as if you were to live forever.'*
>
> Gandhi

LEARN TO WEAR LIFE LIKE A LOOSE GARMENT

The metaphor of 'wearing life like a loose garment' resonated with me many years ago when I noticed I was being controlling, feeling stressed, frustrated, very intense, uptight and not a lot of fun to be around. Life is ever flowing and forever changing. Rather than wearing life like a big heavy winter coat – one that's slightly too small, uncomfortable and a bit restricting – learn to go with the flow and be like water, fit yourself to life, work with what comes up and be flexible.

Wearing life like a loose garment means letting go of the struggle and not holding on so tightly to life that it can't breathe – allowing life its freedom and not trying to bind it up and control it so that it can't move. Wearing life loosely also means following your intuition and changing plans if that feels like the right thing to do – remember, it is OK to change your mind sometimes.

Tuning in to your deeper feelings will give you new insights. Remembering to take time regularly to breathe deeply will bring you into the now, which is where these insights spring from. Wearing life like a loose garment will make it easier for you to take advantage of every opportunity that comes your way. They may be assignments from the universe, so be optimistic and ready for adventure, able to enjoy living in the moment without worrying about the future; able to believe in yourself and be happy to live every day as if it were your last.

CARING FOR YOURSELF

Getting to know how your body works and looking after it as best you can will definitely help you make the most of what you've got. Here are a few basics I keep in mind on a day-to-day basis.

HYDRATE

It's really important to make sure you drink enough water – ideally at least eight to ten glasses a day. Research has shown that doing this can ease back and joint pain, generally increase levels of energy and give you more focus. Not drinking enough water results in headaches and tiredness, has an impact on short-term memory and impedes your ability to do simple calculations. The latest research indicates that even if you only drink five glasses of water each day you'll be reducing the possibility of contracting colon cancer by 45 per cent, breast cancer by 79 per cent and bladder cancer by 50 per cent. Enjoy pure, fresh water often. We're made of it and need to re-hydrate regularly in order to maintain good health.

EAT WELL

Like water, food is essential to our survival. As the primary source of your body's energy it's best to eat the foods that are the freshest and most nutritious. It's also best not to overload your system by eating more than you actually need. Learning to eat slowly and consciously, and properly chewing food in order to maximize your body's absorption of nutrients, will help you listen to your stomach and avoid over-indulging. Allow time between your meals to digest the food you've eaten, and try sipping water to aid digestion. Ideally don't eat just before going to bed, and maintain a healthy, balanced diet, including plenty of fresh fruits and vegetables and sufficient protein, minerals and vitamin-rich foods. Your health and wellbeing depend on it.

SLEEP

Sleep allows the body to repair itself, to power-down in order to recharge its batteries and for the subconscious to process the previous day. Lack of sleep causes all sorts of health problems including depression (poor sleep both precedes depression and is also a symptom of depression) and obesity (a lack of sleep can increase a tendency to overeat). It also leads to poor mental attention. Both the amount of sleep and its quality are important. Experts point to the Internet's 24-hour accessibility as being the primary culprit behind people being distracted from sleeping. If you have sleep difficulties try using my sleep programmes – available from my website or iTunes.

REGULAR EXERCISE

These days it's all too easy to get in the car or on a bus and avoid walking even relatively short distances, but the body's muscles, tendons and ligaments need exercise – so it's use them or lose them. It's important to find a way of getting some kind of regular exercise to increase cardio activity and up your oxygen intake. Ideally you should push your body beyond its normal capacity by doing something you enjoy, whether that's a workout at the gym, cycling, swimming, running, yoga or dancing. It'll oxygenate your brain, increase metabolism, boost your immune system and release 'feel good' chemicals (endorphins) that help to counter depression and anxiety. And if you remain alert and mindful when you exercise you'll enjoy it even more.

PEACE AND QUIET

Many of us live in a fast-paced, constantly moving world where we're surrounded by seemingly endless external distractions – the TV, Internet, people and telephones. All of these may be very welcome when you're a stranger to yourself and not interested in spending quiet time alone, but as you become more and more comfortable with listening to yourself and to simply 'being' without the need for distractions you'll realize the value of quiet for your health, wellbeing, balance and inner peace. It's easier to find when you're around Nature, appreciating the peace and calm while sitting by a tranquil sea, by a river or listening to the wind in the trees. It'll bring you closer to moments of meditation and inner reflection. It's important to try to find moments of peace, quiet and contemplation during the day, and to spend a little less time doing and a little more time being.

13

THINKING YOURSELF WELL

For many years the medical world disputed any link between the mind and the body, but over the last two decades research has increasingly demonstrated that the mind really does have an effect on the body and vice versa. Your body speaks your mind.

Psycho-neuro-immunology – or Mind/Body Medicine – is a relatively new area of medical science that focuses on the relationship between the mind, the nervous system and the immune system.

As I've described before, the mind and body have two lines of communication. One of these is known as the Autonomic Nervous System (ANS). This complex network of nerves and neurons is divided into two branches – the sympathetic and parasympathetic.

The sympathetic system is responsible for the 'fight or flight' response. When it's activated it causes the release of the hormones adrenalin and cortisol – leading to an increase in respiration and heart rate, and the movement of blood away from the body's extremities. When this response kicks in there's a corresponding diminishing of activity in relation to digestion, reproduction and the body's immune system.

The parasympathetic system is responsible for the body relaxing. When activated it slows down our breathing and heart rate, sends blood to our extremities and activates the digestive, reproductive and immune systems.

The other line of mind/body communication is through the Hypothalamus Pituitary Adrenal Axis (or HPA for short). Located in the brain, the hypothalamus and the pituitary glands are involved in regulating chemicals and hormones in the body. Their activity has a direct effect on things like immunity and metabolism.

The latest research shows that what and how we're thinking has a direct impact on the body. Our state of mind also has a close relationship with our immune system. Negative thoughts held in the subconscious mind can make you ill. It's a fact.

THE PLACEBO EFFECT

The power of belief has been proven to be an incredibly potent medicine. Even if there's nothing in the medication given to someone, if they believe there is it can often be as effective as if there actually were. This is called the placebo effect. Placebo treatments can help alleviate a host of health problems from anxiety, depression and pain to inflammatory disorders, Parkinson's disease and even cancer.

A placebo seems to work as a result of the patient's conscious belief in the medication, and their subconscious associations about recovery in similar circumstances. This includes the effects of seeing a doctor in a white coat, or a medical specialist in a clinical environment, and the expectation that recovery will take place. These parallel beliefs seem to subconsciously trigger the body's autoimmune response and the release of hormones which help kickstart the return to improved health.

Modern medicine is beginning to accept that 'What the mind believes, the body achieves.'

LOOKING BACK – DID YOU CHANGE?

I hope you've found that this book has helped you to begin to make the changes needed to start the next stage of your life's important journey.

If you've got to this point in the book – having hopefully done all the exercises and listened regularly to my self-hypnosis programmes – the question I'd like to ask is: did you change or are you in the process of changing?

If the answer is 'yes' then our work together has been a success. If the answer is 'no', was there a part of the process that you didn't want to do? If there was, I urge you to go back and complete it.

If you feel that the process outlined in this book is just too much to do right now; if it somehow overwhelms you, makes you feel uncomfortable or even frightens you, don't worry or be afraid. The exercises are just techniques and guidelines designed to help you *when you're ready*.

If you haven't done so already, I'd recommend that you visit my website and download the hypnosis programmes that accompany this book (www.maxkirsten.com/selfhelpbook). Listening to the downloads regularly for a month will help prepare you and give you the confidence you need to do this important work when you are ready.

If, however, having followed the exercises and practised the techniques you somehow don't feel as good as you were hoping or expecting to feel, don't be disheartened. Sometimes it can take weeks to feel the full benefits. Take heart from knowing that you've done the work as best you could. Remember, this is the beginning of a life's journey. Be patient; the benefits and rewards will come. For some this happens quickly, for others it takes a little more time. What matters is that you're now facing in the right direction and are ready for your unfolding great adventure.

MORE WILL BE REVEALED

By now, if you've been following the exercises and techniques I've outlined in this book:

- Having worked to the best of your ability to clear the wreckage of your past by listing the resentments you've picked up along the way; casting them into the light, along with all your fears and secrets, and begun the lifetime's work of repairing any harm done to others

- Having accepted that we're all flawed and far from perfect, but perfectly imperfect and trying to be the best we can be each day

- Having learnt how to change state naturally from negative to positive at will

- Having found your Self, and in some way perhaps even your connection to the infinite – even though it was never really lost

Hopefully you'll be feeling a lot closer to Nature and realizing that you're as much a part of it as it's a part of you – just like all the other animals, trees, rivers and seas.

Hopefully you're enjoying, respecting and appreciating the differences between us all, feeling able to 'live and let live' and concentrating more on what you're doing to make a difference for others and not so much on what others are doing for you.

And hopefully you're walking a little taller and perhaps with a little more skip in your step, and can look anyone in the eye since it doesn't really matter what they think because you know it's what *you* think about yourself that's more important.

And if you now feel you're heading in the right direction towards becoming the person you imagine you're meant to be, then you're almost certainly on the right path.

And where will that lead to?

Well, that's the great adventure.

More will be revealed.

Appendix 1

A FEW QUESTIONS ABOUT HYPNOSIS

WHAT DOES IT FEEL LIKE TO BE HYPNOTISED?
There is no particular feeling in hypnosis. It can feel relaxing. It probably feels the most like being in a daydream. It's a natural state for us to be in since we all have daydreams. We are in and out of our own little worlds several times a day. In hypnosis we call this state a 'light trance', but in actual fact it's the same as being in a daydream. A common example of this would be if you were driving or riding a bike and you happened to be 'miles away' or in a world of your own and didn't notice the traffic lights had changed from red to green until somebody 'beeped' you. Another is if you were watching a film and got carried away with the characters and almost felt that you were there with them or if you were reading a book and were totally absorbed in the story, imagining all the things you were reading about as if they were really happening. If you're listening to some music and are so absorbed in it you didn't notice it had got dark outside or that time had passed by quite so quickly; if you have ever been in a 'world of your own', or daydream or fantasy, then you've already been in a 'light trance'. You don't need to be in a deep trance-state for this process to work.

HOW MANY TIMES DO I NEED TO LISTEN TO THE HYPNOSIS PROGRAMME THAT COMES WITH THIS BOOK?

Ideally, you should try to listen to the main hypnosis programme every day for a month to achieve the best results.

CAN EVERYONE BE HYPNOTISED?

Yes, as long as you are capable of following simple instructions. The only thing that can stop people going into hypnosis is fear – fear of the unknown or fear of losing control. Hypnosis is a completely natural phenomenon and you're always in control.

WILL I BE ASLEEP?

No. Hypnosis is the Greek word for 'sleep', but you don't actually go to sleep. Hypnosis is a heightened state of awareness (HSA). It's a naturally occurring altered state. However, it's easy to fall asleep in the hypnotic trance-state.

WILL I REMEMBER WHAT HAPPENED?

Yes. You will remember what is said to you.

WILL I LOSE CONTROL?

You are fully aware of everything during the process.

I'M WORRIED I MAY NOT WAKE UP FROM HYPNOSIS.

Being in hypnosis is like being in a 'daydream' or dreaming awake. It's just like you've been resting in a chair, or lying down, without being asleep. Have you ever heard of anyone getting 'stuck' or not waking up from a daydream or a rest? Even if you drift off or fall asleep you would soon return to your usual waking state, just as if you were resting with your eyes closed at any other time. Fact: nobody has ever got 'stuck' while in a hypnotic trance-state.

I FIND IT DIFFICULT TO RELAX; DO I NEED TO RELAX TO BE HYPNOTISED?

No. You don't need to be relaxed in order to be hypnotised. Relaxation is encouraged but not essential.

HOW WILL I KNOW I'M HYPNOTISED?

Most people can't tell the difference between being hypnotised and being in a waking state. Some people feel very relaxed and lethargic, other people feel lightness. One thing that people do notice is an inexplicable change in their daily behaviour afterwards.

DOES IT WORK?

Yes, for most people. Hypnotherapy is the therapeutic use of the hypnotic trance-state. It's NOT a magic wand and nothing can be 100% guaranteed. You must be committed to wanting to change. But as long as you genuinely want to change and are ready to change, hypnotherapy can help you to achieve those changes easily (and sometimes when years of other therapies have failed).

IS IT SAFE?

Yes. Hypnosis is a safe and natural therapy. You can't change your personality or who you really are, but you can change the habits and behaviour patterns that you want to change.

ARE THERE ANY SIDE EFFECTS?

Unlike taking medication, there are no side effects of hypnosis. This is a natural therapy which uses what we already have – the power of our own mind.

WILL HYPNOSIS COMPROMISE MY RELIGIOUS BELIEFS?

There is no reason for it to. Hypnosis works with the power of your own mind to help you make the changes you want. Many people from all sorts of backgrounds and beliefs have benefited from this type of therapy.

Appendix 2

INSPIRATIONAL THOUGHTS

'I searched for God and found only myself. I searched for myself and found only God.'

<small>SUFI PROVERB</small>

'The Self is just our operation centre, our consciousness, our moral compass. So if we want to act more effectively in the world, we have to get to know ourselves better.'

<small>GARY WOLF</small>

'A goal without a date is just a dream.'

<small>MILTON ERICKSON</small>

'*The storms of our life prove the strength of our anchor.*'
AUTHOR UNKNOWN

'*Everything is always created twice, first in your mind then in reality.*'
GANDHI

'*Make your life a mission – not an intermission.*'
ARNOLD GLASGOW

*'Coincidence is God's way of
remaining anonymous.'*
Albert Einstein

*'If a man happens to find himself, he has a
mansion which he can inhabit with dignity all
the days of his life.'*
James Michener

*'Just as a candle cannot burn without fire,
men cannot live without a spiritual life.'*
Buddha

'*Imagination is everything. It is the preview of life's coming attractions.*'

ALBERT EINSTEIN

'*The spirit of self-help is invaluable in making the lives of humans beautiful.*'

RYUHO OKAWA

'*Simplicity is the key to brilliance.*'

BRUCE LEE

'There is but one cause of human failure. And that is man's lack of faith in his true Self.'

WILLIAM JAMES

'In order to know your true self, it is necessary to cast aside your false self.'

RYUHO OKAWA

'My heroes are the ones who survived doing it wrong, who made mistakes but recovered from them.'

BONO

'*Your mind will answer most questions if you learn to relax and wait for the answer.*'
WILLIAM BURROUGHS

'*Happiness is a journey, not a destination. So work like you don't need money, love like you've never been hurt and dance like no one's watching.*'
CRYSTAL BOYD

'*Sometimes I go about in pity for myself. And all the while a great wind carries me across the sky.*'
OJIBWE SAYING

'We cannot become who we need to be by remaining who we are.'
AUTHOR UNKNOWN

'The first step toward change is acceptance. Once you accept yourself, you open the door to change. That's all you have to do. Change is not something you do, it's something you allow.'
WILL GARCIA

'Aim to be someone who will help as many people as possible.'
RYUHO OKAWA

'*Nothing can bring you peace but yourself.*'
RALPH WALDO EMERSON

'*Fear is the opposite of faith.*'
BONO

'*The art of life lies in a constant readjustment to our surroundings.*'
OKAKURA KAKUZO

'*Change will not come if we wait for some other person or some other time.*'

BARACK OBAMA

'*Give thanks for unknown blessings already on their way.*'

NATIVE AMERICAN SAYING

'*Every form of addiction is bad, no matter whether the narcotic be alcohol or morphine or idealism.*'

CARL JUNG

'God, grant me the serenity to accept the things I cannot change, the courage to change the things I can, and the wisdom to know the difference.'

REINHOLD NIEBUHR

The Man Who Thinks He Can

If you think you're beaten, you are
If you think you dare not, you don't
If you'd like to win, but think you can't,
It's almost a cinch you won't.
If you think you'll lose, you've lost
For out in the world we find
Success being with a fellow's will
It's all in the state of mind.
If you think you're outclassed, you are;
You've got to think high to rise
You've got to be sure of yourself
Before you can ever win a prize.
Life's battles don't always go
To the stronger or faster man;
But soon or late, the one who wins
Is the man who thinks he can.

WALTER D WINTLE

'*The master in the art of living makes little distinction between his work and his play, his labour and his leisure, his mind and his body, his information and his recreation, his love and his religion. He hardly knows which is which. He simply pursues his vision of excellence at whatever he does, leaving others to decide whether he is working or playing. To him he's always doing both.*'

AN UNKNOWN ZEN MASTER

'*Keep your thoughts positive because your thoughts become your words. Keep your words positive because your words become your behaviours. Keep your behaviours positive because your behaviours become your habits. Keep your habits positive because your habits become your values. Keep your values positive because your values become your destiny.*'

GANDHI

Our Deepest Fear

Our deepest fear is not that we are inadequate
Our deepest fear is that we are powerful
beyond measure
It is our light, not our darkness
that most frightens us
We ask ourselves, who am I to be brilliant,
gorgeous, talented, fabulous?
Actually, who are you not to be?
You are a child of God
Your playing small does not serve the world
There is nothing enlightened about shrinking so
that other people won't feel insecure around you
We are all meant to shine, as children do
We were born to make manifest the glory of
God that is within us.
It is not just in some of us; it is in everyone
And as we let our own light shine,
we unconsciously give other people permission
to do the same
As we are liberated from our own fear, our
presence automatically liberates others

MARIANNE WILLIAMSON

Just for Today

Just for today I will try to live through this day only and not tackle my whole life problem at once. I can do something for 12 hours that would appal me if I felt that I had to keep it up for a lifetime.

Just for today I will be happy. Most folks are as happy as they make up their minds to be.

Just for today I will adjust myself to what is and not try to adjust everything else to my desires. I will take my 'luck' as it comes and fit myself into it.

Just for today I will try to strengthen my mind. I will study; I will learn something useful; I will not be a mental loafer; I will read something that requires effort, thought and concentration.

Just for today I will exercise my soul in three ways: I will do somebody a good turn and not get found out; if anybody knows of it, it will not count; I will do at least two things I don't want to do – just for exercise. I will not show anyone that my feelings are hurt; they may be hurt, but today I will not show it.

Just for today I will be agreeable. I will look as good as I can, dress becomingly, talk low, act courteously, criticize not one bit, not find fault with anything and not try to improve or regulate anybody except myself.

Just for today I will have a programme. I may not follow it exactly, but I will have it. I will save myself from two pests: hurry and indecision.

Just for today I will have a quiet half hour all by myself and relax. During this half hour, sometime, I will try to get a better perspective on my life.

Just for today I will be unafraid. I will enjoy that which is beautiful and will believe that as I give to the world, so the world will give to me.

Appearing in a 1940s self-help book: *How to Stop Worrying and Start Living* by Dale Carnegie, the text on which Alcoholics Anonymous UK's 'Just for Today' card is based was originally written by Sibyl F Partridge in the early 20th century.

Appendix 3

THE 12 STEPS OF
ALCOHOLICS ANONYMOUS

12-step programmes are well-known for use in recovery from addictive or dysfunctional behaviours. The first 12-Step programme began with Alcoholics Anonymous (AA) in the 1930s. The 12-step approach has since grown to be the most widely used approach in dealing with not only alcoholism but also drug abuse and various other addictive or dysfunctional behaviours.

THE 12 STEPS ADAPTED FOR ADDICTIONS AND DYSFUNCTIONAL BEHAVIOURS

Step 1 – We admitted we were powerless over our addiction – that our lives had become unmanageable

Step 2 – Came to believe that a Power greater than ourselves could restore us to sanity

Step 3 – Made a decision to turn our will and our lives over to the care of God as we understand God

Step 4 – Made a searching and fearless moral inventory of ourselves

Step 5 – Admitted to God, to ourselves and to another human being the exact nature of our wrongs

Step 6 – Were entirely ready to have God remove all these defects of character

Step 7 – Humbly asked God to remove our shortcomings

Step 8 – Made a list of all persons we had harmed, and became willing to make amends to them all

Step 9 – Made direct amends to such people wherever possible, except when to do so would injure them or others

Step 10 – Continued to take personal inventory and when we were wrong promptly admitted it

Step 11 – Sought through prayer and meditation to improve our conscious contact with God as we understand God, praying only for knowledge of God's will for us and the power to carry that out

Step 12 – Having had a spiritual awakening as the result of these steps, we tried to carry this message to other addicts, and to practise these principles in all our affairs

The original 12 steps of AA are the basis of the most powerful self-improvement programme in the world and have already helped millions of people. They have been described as one of the 'greatest social movements of the 20th century'.

THE 12 STEPS OF ALCOHOLICS ANONYMOUS

Step 1 – We admitted we were powerless over alcohol – that our lives had become unmanageable

Step 2 – Came to believe that a Power greater than ourselves could restore us to sanity

Step 3 – Made a decision to turn our will and our lives over to the care of God as we understand Him

Step 4 – Made a searching and fearless moral inventory of ourselves

Step 5 – Admitted to God, to ourselves and to another human being the exact nature of our wrongs

Step 6 – Were entirely ready to have God remove all these defects of character

Step 7 – Humbly asked Him to remove our shortcomings

Step 8 – Made a list of all persons we had harmed, and became willing to make amends to them all

Step 9 – Made direct amends to such people wherever possible, except when to do so would injure them or others

Step 10 – Continued to take personal inventory and when we were wrong promptly admitted it

Step 11 – Sought through prayer and meditation to improve our conscious contact with God as we understand Him, praying only for knowledge of His will for us and the power to carry that out

Step 12 – Having had a spiritual awakening as the result of these steps, we tried to carry this message to alcoholics and to practise these principles in all our affairs

The Twelve Steps of Alcoholics Anonymous are reprinted and adapted with permission of Alcoholics Anonymous World Services, Inc. ('AAWS'). Permission to adapt the Twelve Steps does not mean that AAWS has reviewed or approved the contents of this publication, or that AAWS necessarily agrees with the views expressed herein. AA is a programme of recovery from alcoholism *only* – use of the Twelve Steps in connection with programmes and activities which are patterned after AA, but which address other problems, or in any other non-AA context, does not imply otherwise.

THE SPIRITUAL PRINCIPLES OF THE 12 STEPS:

1. Honesty
2. Acceptance
3. Surrender
4. Hope
5. Commitment
6. Faith
7. Courage
8. Willingness
9. Humility
10. Unconditional love
11. Perseverance
12. Open-mindedness
13. God-centeredness
14. Awareness
15. Vigilance
16. Self-discipline
17. Sharing and caring
18. Patience
19. Forgiveness
20. Optimism
21. Selflessness
22. Compassion
23. Consideration
24. Kindness
25. Positive thinking
26. Responsibility
27. Tolerance
28. Trust
29. Unity
30. Gratitude
31. Service

USEFUL RESOURCES

12-STEP PROGRAMMES

ALCOHOLICS ANONYMOUS
http://www.aa.org/
Alcoholics Anonymous is a fellowship of men and women who share their experiences and strength, and the hope that they may solve their common problem and help others recover from alcoholism.

NARCOTICS ANONYMOUS
http://www.na.org/
Narcotics Anonymous is an international, community-based association of drug addicts with more than 31,000 weekly meetings in over 100 countries.

COCAINE ANONYMOUS
http://www.ca.org/
Cocaine Anonymous is a fellowship of men and women who share their experience, strength and hope with each other so that they may solve their common problem and help others to recover from their addiction.

AL-ANON
http://www.al-anon.org/
This organization helps families and friends of alcoholics recover from the effects of living with the problem drinking of a relative or friend.

ALATEEN
http://www.al-anon.org/alateen.html
Alateen is a recovery programme for young people. Alateen groups are sponsored by Al-Anon members.

NAR-ANON – FAMILIES ANONYMOUS IN THE UK!
http://www.nar-anon.org/
The Nar-Anon Family Group is primarily for those who know or have known a feeling of desperation concerning the addiction problem of someone very near to them. They have travelled that unhappy road, too, and have found the answer with serenity and peace of mind.

OVEREATERS ANONYMOUS (OA)
http://www.oa.org/
Overeaters Anonymous offers a programme of recovery from compulsive overeating using the 12 Steps and 12 Traditions of OA.

GAMBLERS ANONYMOUS
http://www.gamblersanonymous.org
Gamblers Anonymous is a fellowship of men and women who share their experience, strength and hope with each other so that they might solve their common problem and help others to recover from a gambling addiction.

DEBTORS ANONYMOUS
http://www.debtorsanonymous.org/
Is your life unmanageable because of credit card debt and overspending? Debtors Anonymous offers a programme of recovery.

NICOTINE ANONYMOUS
http://www.nicotine-anonymous.org/
Nicotine Anonymous is a non-profit 12-step fellowship of men and women helping each other live nicotine-free lives.

EMOTIONS ANONYMOUS
http://www.emotionsanonymous.org/
Emotions Anonymous is a 12-step organization similar to Alcoholics Anonymous. This fellowship is composed of people who come together in weekly meetings for the purpose of working towards recovery from emotional difficulties.

CRYSTAL METH ANONYMOUS
http://www.crystalmeth.org/
Crystal Meth Anonymous is a fellowship of men and women for whom all drugs, specifically Crystal Meth, have become a problem.

DEPRESSED ANONYMOUS
http://www.depressedanon.com/
Depressed Anonymous was formed to provide therapeutic resources for depressed individuals of all ages.

HCV ANONYMOUS
http://www.hcvanonymous.com/
HCV Anonymous exists to assist hepatitis patients and their loved ones in taking control of their spiritual, physical, mental, and emotional health by providing current, comprehensive information in one source.

OBSESSIVE COMPULSIVE ANONYMOUS
http://obsessivecompulsiveanonymous.org/
This is a fellowship of people who share their experience, strength and hope with each other so that they may solve their common problem and help others to recover from OCD.

RECOVERING COUPLES ANONYMOUS
http://www.recovering-couples.org/
The primary purpose of RCA is to help couples find freedom from dysfunctional patterns in relationships.

CO-DEPENDENTS ANONYMOUS
http://www.coda.org/
Co-Dependents Anonymous is a fellowship of men and women whose common purpose is to develop healthy relationships. The only requirement for membership is a desire for healthy and loving relationships.

SEX AND LOVE ADDICTS ANONYMOUS
http://www.slaauk.com/
Sex and Love Addicts Anonymous is a 12-step/12 Tradition-oriented fellowship based on the model pioneered by Alcoholics Anonymous.

FAMILIES ANONYMOUS
http://www.familiesanonymous.org/
Families Anonymous is a group of concerned relatives and friends who have faced up to the reality that the problems of someone close to them are seriously affecting their lives and ability to function normally.

ANOREXICS AND BULIMICS ANONYMOUS
http://www.anorexicsandbulimicsanonymousaba.com/
ABA uses the 12-step programme adapted from Alcoholics Anonymous to address the mental, emotional and spiritual components of the disorders of anorexia and bulimia. By following the 12 steps they work towards a deep level of freedom from deadly obsessions with body weight and shape and with food, obsessions that once dominated their minds and dictated the course of their lives.

WORKAHOLICS ANONYMOUS
http://www.workaholics-anonymous.org/
Workaholics Anonymous is a fellowship of individuals who share their experience, strength and hope with each other so that they may solve their common problems and help others to recover from workaholism.

TOP TREATMENT CENTRES FOR ADDICTION

COTTONWOOD TUCSON
www.cottonwooddetucson.com
Addiction treatment and drug rehabilitation at Cottonwood Tucson in Tucson, Arizona, USA. Cottonwood Tucson is a world-renowned centre for people suffering from alcoholism and drug addiction.

THE MEADOWS
http://www.themeadows.org
The Meadows in Wickenburg, Arizona is one of the world's top treatment centres for addictions, both substance (alcohol, drugs, food, etc.) and process (gambling, work, sex, Internet, etc.) and childhood abuse. The Meadows places a strong emphasis on successful 12-step programmes.

CROSSROADS CENTRE AT ANTIGUA
http://www.crossroadsantigua.org/
Crossroads Centre is a non-profit international centre of excellence for the treatment of alcohol and other drug addictions. The programme was founded by Eric Clapton on the beautiful island of Antigua, West Indies. Residential and outpatient services are provided within a 12-step framework while integrating key complementary therapies to provide a whole-person approach to treatment and ongoing recovery.

CLOUDS HOUSE REHAB CLINIC
http://www.actiononaddiction.org.uk/
Set in a naturally therapeutic environment of beautiful Wiltshire parkland, Clouds has been helping people with addiction problems for 25 years. In a beautiful and safe environment you can begin to understand your own true potential and build a new life without drugs or alcohol. Clouds offers a well-structured treatment programme for you to learn about yourself in relation to addiction, your vulnerability to relapse and how you can sustain recovery by working with the 12-step abstinence-based philosophy.

PROMIS REHAB CLINICS
http://www.promis.co.uk/
Promis has over 25 years' experience of helping patients recover from the challenges of addiction and other concurrent disorders. Whether you need to seek addiction treatment for yourself or a loved one, you will find that all Promis clinics offer a peaceful setting that is family orientated. With locations across Europe, open 24/7, Promis offers immediate admission.

THE PRIORY
www.priorygroup.com
The Priory Hospital Roehampton, west London, and the the Priory Hospital Southgate, north London, are both private independent hospitals, specializing in the management and treatment of mental health problems including addictions and eating disorders. Free confidential assessment at your nearest Priory hospital for all addictions, including alcohol, drugs, gambling, shopping and computer.

RECOMMENDED READING

Calvin D Banyan and Gerald F Kein, *Hypnosis and Hypnotherapy: Basic to Advanced Techniques for the Professional* (Abbot Publishing House Inc.)

Deirdre Bounds, *Fulfilled: A Personal Revolution in Seven Steps* (Pearson Prentice Hall)

Mihaly Csikszentmihalyi, *Flow: The Classic Work on How to Achieve Happiness* (Rider)

His Holiness the Dalai Lama and Howard C. Cutler, *The Art of Happiness: A Handbook for Living* (Coronet)

Dave Elman, *Hypnotherapy* (Westwood Publishing)

Malcolm Gladwell, *Blink: The Power of Thinking Without Thinking* (Penguin)

Malcolm Gladwell, *Outliers: The Story of Success* (Penguin)

Thich Nhat Hanh, *The Miracle of Mindfulness: The Classic Guide to Meditation by the World's Most Revered Master* (Classic Edition; Rider)

Robert Holden, *Success Intelligence: Essential Lessons and Practices from the World's leading Coaching Programme on Authentic Success* (Hodder Mobius)

Carl Honore, *In Praise of Slow: How a Worldwide Movement is Challenging the Cult of Speed* (Orion Books)

Byron Katie and Stephen Mitchell, *Loving What Is: How Four Questions Can Change Your Life* (Rider)

Dennis Genpo Merzel, *The Path of the Human Being: Zen Teachings on the Bodhisattva Way* (Shambhala)

M Scott Peck, *The Road Less Travelled: A New Psychology of Love, Traditional Values and Spiritual Growth* (Rider Random House)

Richard H Thaler and Cass R Sunstein, *Nudge: Improving Decisions About Health, Wealth and Happiness* (Penguin)

Eckhart Tolle, *A New Earth: Create a Better Life* (Penguin)

Daidoji Yuzan, Oscar Ratti and Thomas Cleary, *The Code of the Samurai: A Modern Translation of the Bushido Shoshinshu of Taira Shigesuke* (Tuttle Publishing)

NOTES

NOTES

NOTES

NOTES

Hay House Titles of Related Interest

A Deep Breath of Life,
by Alan Cohen

Happiness Now,
by Robert Holden

Life Lessons,
by Lesley Garner

One-Minute Mindfulness,
by Simon Parke

SuperCoach,
by Michael Neill

Waking from Sleep,
by Steve Taylor

Why Kindness Is Good for You,
by David R. Hamilton

MAX KIRSTEN'S HYPNOTHERAPY NLP 'LIFE CHANGE' APPS

Quit Smoking Now

Weight Loss Now

Relax Now

The ABC of Better Sleep

The Insomnia Cure

Max's hypnotherapy NLP apps are available for the iPhone, iPad, iPod Touch, iPod Classic and on all mobile devices. They are available from iTunes, Amazon, Audible.com and in MP3 format from **www.maxkirsten.com**

Visit Max's website **www.maxkirsten.com** for regular self-help advice and updates.

To download the hypnotic program that Max has created to accompany this book, visit **www.maxkirsten.com/selfhelpbook**

THE
CLEAR PROCESS

Becoming the person you want to be – taking care of yourself – learning to let your Self take care of you.

Max has distilled the essential components of his unique approach to self-help and personal transformation into a dynamic two-day programme. Join Max for a powerful 'Life Change' weekend: learn the art and practice of self-hypnosis, cure yourself of the disease of Moreism, develop your ability to use the power of Breathing Plus, and master your capacity for living in the present moment, experiencing the extraordinariness of the SuperNow!

Visit **www.maxkirsten.com/theclearprocess** for details and dates of forthcoming weekends when you too can experience **The Clear Process™**.

JOIN THE HAY HOUSE FAMILY

As the leading self-help, mind, body and spirit publisher in the UK, we'd like to welcome you to our family so that you can enjoy all the benefits our website has to offer.

 EXTRACTS from a selection of your favourite author titles

 COMPETITIONS, PRIZES & SPECIAL OFFERS Win extracts, money off, downloads and so much more

 LISTEN to a range of radio interviews and our latest audio publications

 CELEBRATE YOUR BIRTHDAY An inspiring gift will be sent your way

 LATEST NEWS Keep up with the latest news from and about our authors

 **ATTEND OUR AUTHOR EVENTS** Be the first to hear about our author events

 **iPHONE APPS** Download your favourite app for your iPhone

 HAY HOUSE INFORMATION Ask us anything, all enquiries answered

join us online at **www.hayhouse.co.uk**

 292B Kensal Road, London W10 5BE
T: 020 8962 1230 E: info@hayhouse.co.uk